M000290319

Advance praise

"*Catholic and Confident* is a valuable, practical, easy-to-read wake-up call for the new evangelization. An excellent handbook for pastors, evangelization committees, small groups, RCIA, and all parishioners who want to know the why and how of sharing our faith."

—Msgr. Michael Eivers, pastor, St. Edward Parish

"Henry Libersat knows the man who gave the Sermon on the Mount, and he has a way of sharing Christ's message in greetings and conversations, in banter and even in jokes. That's a kind of personal evangelism that many of us Christians want to practice. In *Catholic and Confident*, Deacon Libersat offers simple lessons in evangelism. He shows that indeed we can do what Jesus did."

—A.E.P. Wall, past editor of Catholic News Service
and author of *The Spirit of Cardinal Bernadin*

"In *Catholic and Confident*, Henry Libersat goes deep into the *mystery* of our faith and of Christian living. He doesn't scare us off; he slips in mystery so gently it is almost unnoticed. Unnoticed—but not ignored. In fact, nothing in this book should be ignored. This is a book that should be, not on every shelf, but in every heart. Read it!"

—Fr. David Knight

"In this book, Henry's goal is to help us become disciples who can win and form other disciples. He plots out for us the pattern of our growth to maturity in Christ, which is the ground of all evangelization efforts."

—Bert Ghezzi, author of *Adventures in Daily Prayer*

"I recommend Deacon Henry Libersat's book, *Catholic and Confident*, to all Catholics who are genuinely interested in the faith, but especially to those concerned with evangelizing a world that is desperate for direction in life. Henry, in his own inimitable way takes on the challenge of the Church for the future and invites others to join him.

—Fr. Michael Burke, St. Joseph's Cathedral

"I have known Henry Libersat for forty years. He has been consistent in his desire and ability to attract people into a closer relationship with God. He makes our faith exciting and desirable. *Catholic and Confident* is darned good—no, it is excellent! It deserves to be read."

—Lee Callaghan, foundress of Spirit of God Community
and author of *The Gospel According to Mom*

"*Catholic and Confident* by Henry Libersat is immensely readable. It will certainly whet the appetite of anyone interested in evangelization and rekindle ardor in the most seasoned evangelist. For Libersat, evangelization is relational. It begins by intimately knowing the Father's love. It grows in the attention to people encountered each day, and in proclaiming faith as an expression of love. Using the power of story, Libersat seeks to empower all Catholics for evangelization. His passion and enthusiasm for evangelization shine through, supported by his vast experience."

—Rev. Michael Hurley, Pioneer of Parish Cell System
of Evangelization in Ireland

CATHOLIC
AND
CONFIDENT

Simple Steps to Share Your Faith

HENRY LIBERSAT

SERVANT
BOOKS

PUBLISHED BY FRANCISCAN MEDIA
Cincinnati, Ohio

Cover design by John Lucas
Cover image © Ron Fehling | Masterfile
Book design by Mark Sullivan

LIBRARY OF CONGRESS CATALOGING-IN-PUBLICATION DATA
Libersat, Henry.
Catholic and confident : simple steps to share your faith / Henry Libersat.
p. cm.
Includes bibliographical references (p.   ).
ISBN 978-1-61636-428-1 (alk. paper)
1. Evangelistic work—Catholic Church. 2. Witness bearing (Christianity)—Catholic Church. 3. Catholic Church—Doctrines. I. Title.
BX2347.4.L53 2012
248'.5—dc23
2012011457

ISBN 978-1-61636-428-1

Published by Servant Books, an imprint of
Franciscan Media
28 W. Liberty St.
Cincinnati, OH 45202
www.FranciscanMedia.org
www.ServantBooks.org

Printed in the United States of America.
Printed on acid-free paper.

12 13 14 15 16   5 4 3 2 1

CONTENTS

ACKNOWLEDGMENTS

Throughout my life many people have been very good to me. I would be remiss, however, if I did not thank the following wonderful people.

My wife, Peg, supports me in love and ministry. She sits alone in church while I function as a deacon. She put up with my alcohol-induced Jekyll-and-Hyde personality for twenty-two years and puts up with me still.

My parents, Henry and Elda, now with the Lord, gave me life, love, and education. Most of all they made our Catholic faith the foundation of my life.

Several priests must be mentioned: David P. Page, and the late Frs. Alexander O. Sigur and Charles B. Fortier, who guided me through forty years of active Catholic newspaper work; and the late Msgr. Georges A. Levasseur, a tremendous spiritual director who often reminded me, "When you fall flat on your face, you are still pointed in the same direction. Lift your face out of the mud and see the crucified hand of Christ ready to lift you up."

The three bishops of the Orlando diocese, under whom I labored at *The Florida Catholic*, were inspiring and supportive: the late Archbishop William D. Borders, first bishop of Orlando; the late Bishop Thomas J. Grady, second bishop of Orlando; and Bishop Norbert M. Dorsey, C.P., third bishop of Orlando.

Bert Ghezzi, a dear brother and friend, joins me in leading our Monday morning men's Bible study. His guidance in the writing of this book gave me direction and inspiration. Also Claudia Volkman of Servant Books encouraged me when the process seemed too long to my get-it-done-yesterday mentality.

And last but not least, I want to thank two parish priests who have been in my life for more than twenty years: Fr. Charles I. Mitchell, pastor, and Msgr. Edward Thompson, both at St. Mary Magdalen Church in Altamonte Springs, Florida. These two men preach great homilies and promote the ministry of all people in the parish. They are especially supportive of the diaconal ministry, which I share with three brother deacons at St. Mary Magdalen—Marshall Gibbs, Gerry Kelly, and Juan Cruz.

FOREWORD

For half a century popes have been exhorting and encouraging all Catholics to take up their responsibility for evangelization. Pope John Paul II, for example, called for a New Evangelization that would generate a "springtime" of sharing the faith. He wanted laypeople in particular to proclaim the Good News to their families and neighbors and the persons next to them in the pew.[1]

But many Catholics still do not evangelize. Some think that it's a Protestant thing. Others have misconceptions about evangelization, imagining that it means passing out tracts or preaching on street corners. And sadly, most Catholics have not heard the popes' appeals and are still unaware of their duty to share the faith.

Henry Libersat, himself an active evangelizer, has been urging Catholics to evangelize for longer than I have known him. And we have been friends for more than twenty-five years. He has shown by example that growing in the Lord through prayer, Scripture study, and participation in the sacraments—especially the Eucharist—prepares us for sharing the Good News. He teaches that genuine evangelization means drawing others to Christ and the Church by reaching out to them in friendship and service. I have learned many things from him, but most of all I value his challenging me to persevere in trying to win the hearts of slow-to-respond family members and friends.

I am delighted that Henry decided to put his vision and wisdom in a book in order to stir us couch-potato Catholics to get off our duffs and embrace our privileged duty to evangelize. In a gentle, nonthreatening style, he disabuses us of inadequate ideas about evangelization. Out of his own experience and the experiences of others, he demonstrates what it really involves.

Henry's goal is to help us become disciples who can win and form other disciples. He leads us to enter into a personal relationship with Christ, an intimate connection with the Lord that will drive our Christian lives. He shows us how to listen for God's call. Henry then plots out for us our growth to maturity in Christ, which is the ground of all evangelization efforts.

For those who have never evangelized, Henry explains how to get started. And he tells the stories of numerous ordinary Catholics just like us who successfully share the Good News in their everyday lives. I was especially touched by the story of Jim Seibert, whose persistent and kind friendliness persuaded Butch, an AIDS victim, to give his life to Christ moments before he died.

Henry assures us that we can lead others to Christ and the Church because we have received the Holy Spirit. And the Spirit gives us a great diversity of transformational and spiritual gifts that equip us for the work of evangelization.

Henry truly demonstrates the why and how of evangelization. So be Catholic. Be confident. Let's join him in doing what Jesus did.

—Bert Ghezzi

INTRODUCTION

On Sunday mornings, I arrive with my wife, Peg, at St. Mary Magdalen Church in Altamonte Springs, Florida, at 8:00 AM. Peg attends Mass at that hour; I usually assist as deacon at the 10:00 AM Mass, so during the 8:00 AM Mass, I sit in the sacristy for my morning prayer and listen to the homily. Then I walk over to the rectory to await the priests and other deacons for breakfast. It's one of the few times we manage to get together for a little fellowship along with lay cantors and a nun who serves as sacristan.

One Sunday morning I sat in the rectory living room, reflecting on our parish, the Church in general, and my life in particular. At seventy-six years of age, I felt frustrated because so many people were leaving or never entering our Catholic Church. I suppose I was praying a bit, asking God what to do about evangelization, for which I've always had a passion. A quiet voice spoke clearly: "Write a book."

Excitement flooded me. I had written several books, but I thought those days were over. I still sent out e-mail reflections: a monthly "Way, Truth, and Life" and an occasional "Of Wine and Gall" and "Brothers in the Lord." The latter goes to the men in our Monday-morning Bible study and to the men who gather monthly for Scripture study in a ministry they have dubbed ACTS 29. I host a blog—www.HenryLibersat.com and have also succumbed to Facebook.

A possible title of the book came to me: *You Can Do What Jesus Did* because what he did was bring the message of the Father's love to all humanity. What he did was live among us and teach us, by word and example, what it means to know and love God. He died so we might have eternal life. We, too, must witness to and preach God's love, die to self for the sake of others, and lead them to the foot of the cross to discover the depths of God's love for them.

My friend Bert Ghezzi asked me two very practical questions: "Why do you want to write this book? And what is its goal?" After some prayerful thought I came up with this—the reason and the goal: *To convince Catholics that they are called by God to share their faith and that they have the grace and power to do so.*

Happily, the publisher came up with the perfect book title: *Catholic and Confident: Simple Steps to Share Your Faith.*

That's how this work began. And now here it is. In these pages may you find inspiration, consolation, and confirmation of your value to the mission of Christ.

PART ONE

The Foundation for Sharing Faith

I no longer call you slaves, because a slave does not know what his master is doing. I have called you friends, because I have told you everything I have heard from my Father. It was not you who chose me, but I who chose you and appointed you to go out and bear fruit that will remain, so that whatever you ask the Father in my name he may give you.

—John 15:15–16

The renewal of the Church is also achieved through the witness offered by the lives of believers: by their very existence in the world, Christians are called to radiate the word of truth that the Lord Jesus left us.

—Pope Benedict XVI, *Porta Fidei*, 6

CHAPTER ONE

God
Is
Calling
You

Do not conform yourself to this age but be transformed by the renewal of your mind, that you may discern what is the will of God, what is good and pleasing and perfect.

—Romans 12:2

In earlier days Catholic evangelization was considered primarily the work of priests and other religious. These people brought God's love to foreign lands, including the Americas. That was good! These priests and religious—many of whom were martyred for their faith—did wonderful work and brought millions into the Church.

But now, in the twenty-first century, God asks you, a layperson—young or old, married or single—to bring the Good News of salvation to everyone in your life: to your family, the people at work, and those you meet while shopping, sitting in your doctor's office, coaching sports, or standing outside church before and after Sunday Mass.

The Second Vatican Council made this clear:

> The laity...are given this special vocation: to make the Church present and fruitful in those places and circumstances where

it is only through them that she can become the salt of the earth. Thus, every lay person, through those gifts given to him [or her], is at once the witness and the living instrument of the mission of the Church....

—*Dogmatic Constitution on the Church*, 33

...The laity become powerful heralds of the faith in things to be hoped for (cf. Hebrews 11:1) if they join unhesitating profession of faith to the life of faith. This evangelization, that is, the proclamation of Christ by word and the testimony of life, acquires a specific property and peculiar efficacy because it is accomplished in the ordinary circumstances of the world....

Therefore, even when occupied by temporal affairs, the laity can, and must, do valuable work for the evangelization of the world.

—*Dogmatic Constitution on the Church*, 33, 35

Laypeople are the ones now mainly responsible for evangelizing. At baptism we began our life as disciples of Christ. We were filled with the Holy Spirit, the Lord and giver of life. We were made one with God. We share his divine life. We have the right, duty, and power to tell people about salvation through Jesus Christ.

"But," you may object, "I am unprepared. I don't know Scripture that well, or theology."

It is love of God and neighbor, rather than academic degrees, which brings people to Christ and his Church. This duty and privilege is for all Catholics. No one is excused from the Great Commission of Jesus: "Go, therefore, and make disciples of all nations, baptizing them in the name of the Father, and of the Son, and of the Holy Spirit, teaching them to observe everything I have commanded you" (Matthew 28:19a).

There is no one else like you. There is no one else in the world who is where you are in relation to those in your life and to those you meet even casually during the day. You are essential to God's work among his people.

GOD'S AGENTS

You may find the word *evangelization* a bit scary. Perhaps it brings to mind unsettling scenes of people shoving tracts in your face or shouting about God and fear and damnation. Maybe you have seen people walking down the street and "preaching" through a bullhorn. Or maybe you think of TV evangelists fleecing their viewers.

Effective evangelization is not any of these things. There is no need for shouting, for casting fear upon the masses. True evangelization relies on God's love and the truth and power of his Word. It is both gentle and friendly. Blessed Pope John Paul II's New Evangelization is at first directed not at the unbelievers "out there" but at anyone who has not been fully converted and catechized—people in our own families, members of our parishes, and Catholics in particular movements and professions in which Christian witness is sorely needed.

When we share our faith, Jesus is our model. He had compassion on the unbeliever. He met people on their own level, and he spoke their language—in parables and stories they could understand.

The way you evangelize is solidly rooted in the way you live and relate to other people. You are an agent through which God will reach others. Larry Puccio offers a good example of true Catholic evangelizing.

Larry is a plumber living in Pembroke Pines, Florida. He has been a Catholic his entire life, but when his wife converted to Catholicism, her enthusiasm and knowledge of Christ led him closer to God. He and Lynn are active at St. Edward, a parish committed to evangelization, especially of people in the pew. No surprise that Larry has picked up the "faith-sharing bug." And he shares his faith in a friendly and effective way.

"When I am out on a job," he explains, "I pray for the opportunity to tell people about my faith in Christ and about our Church." At a customer's house he may see a picture of a scene from Europe or portraits of family members or of other persons important to the household. "I ask the owners about the pictures—'Were you in Europe?' Or, 'Is that your father?'—and we share a bit about our families and experiences. I'll mention how important my parish is to me and how faith in God has enriched my life. If they are open to further sharing, we go for it."

Whoever and whatever you are—housewife or career woman, farmer or grocer, laborer or banker, police officer or soldier—you are called to evangelize, to help people discover the great peace in coming to know Jesus and live in the Church, the family of God.

You already affect other people. You already help them. How can you incorporate that into the greatest help possible—bringing them to know Jesus?

If your relationship with Jesus Christ is genuine, it will show. People will see you celebrate something wonderful with them as well as mourning with them in their grief and comforting them. Being a friend, one who empathizes and supports, is the first step in helping people discover the secret to your happiness—an intimate union with Jesus Christ, your Lord and Savior.

> ...Evangelizing means bringing the Good News of Jesus into every human situation and seeking to convert individuals and society by the divine power of the Gospel itself.
>
> —United States Conference of Catholic Bishops[2]

IT'S ALL ABOUT JESUS

When you share faith with others, you have to start with Jesus. He is the one "who comes in the name of the Lord" (Matthew 21:9), the one who reconciles us with the Father (see 2 Corinthians 5:18). He is the Way into the joy and strength of faith, the Truth that is God's love, and the Life that restlessly seeks the heart of each and every person on earth.

> At [evangelization's] essence are the proclamation of salvation in Jesus Christ and the response of a person in faith, both of which are the works of the Spirit of God.
>
> Evangelization must always be directly connected to the Lord Jesus Christ. "There is no true evangelization if the name, the teaching, the life, the promises, the Kingdom and the mystery of Jesus of Nazareth, the Son of God, are not proclaimed."
>
> —United States Conference of Catholic Bishops[3]

God wants all people to be saved. He fills us with his Holy Spirit—to guide and inspire us, to give us insight, wisdom, and courage. In baptism we were marked with the priestly character of Christ himself. We were called to do what Jesus did. Vatican Council II summed it up in these words:

> There are innumerable opportunities open to the laity for the exercise of their apostolate of evangelization and sanctification. The very testimony of their Christian life and good works done in a supernatural spirit have the power to draw men to belief and to God; for the Lord says, "Even so let your light shine

before men in order that they may see your good works and give glory to your Father who is in heaven" (Matthew 5:16).

—*Decree on the Apostolate of the Laity*, 6

It is crystal clear: You are called to do what Jesus did. And you can.

FOR REFLECTION

- How would you define authentic Catholic evangelism?
- Why do you, as a layperson, have to be concerned with evangelization?
- What are some ways you can begin today to share the Good News with those around you?

CHAPTER TWO

Finding Jesus

I am the vine, you are the branches. Whoever remains in me
and I in him will bear much fruit, because without me you can
do nothing.

—John 15:5

Cardinal Peter Turkson, of Cape Coast, Africa, was interviewed
by *The Times* of London in 2007. He said, in part, that
coming to know Christ as Savior and Lord calls for a radical
conversion.[4] I understand this radical conversion as leaping beyond the
comfort zone in which we keep Jesus in the tabernacle and between the
covers of the Bible.

Coming to know your Lord and Savior is a lifelong process. No one
ever gets to the "end" of Jesus. If you want to help others come to the
Lord, you need to understand the process through which people must
move.

You've probably read or heard the story of the man born blind (see
John 9:1–40). It gives us some insight into how you and I, and the
people we evangelize, come to know Jesus personally and intimately.
You may want to take a moment to read this passage for yourself and
then follow along with me.

LESSONS FROM A BLIND MAN

I see three movements or stages the blind man experienced as he came to know Jesus.

First, awareness. This is the first step of God's call. The person somehow becomes aware of Jesus—through parents, a friend, or an overheard discussion. The result might be a somewhat tentative curiosity. The person begins to wonder about Jesus. Then, in one way or another—maybe through prayer, being healed, or a new interest in Scripture—the person feels his presence. Jesus is real and really there.

In the Gospels it seems that Jesus became aware of the blind man before the blind man became aware of Jesus: "As he passed by he saw a man blind from birth" (John 9:1). It's comforting to know that Jesus knows about us way before we know about him. But perhaps the blind man had heard about Jesus already. Jesus had healed others—the official's son and the man at the Sheep Gate (see John 4:46–54; 5:1–16). He had changed water into wine, fed the five thousand, and walked on the sea (John 2:1–11; 6:1–21).

The disciples, too, played a part. They asked Jesus why the man was born blind (John 9:2). This led to the blind man's becoming aware of Jesus in a pretty dramatic way: Jesus healed him!

Second, recognition. The man, when called before the angry Jewish leaders, recognized the power of Jesus because he had been healed. He also discerned that this healer could not be evil, that he had to be a good man, one who was from God (see John 9:33).

This moment of recognition is common to new believers. Jesus is more than they at first believed or understood. They are attracted to him.

We Christians continue to experience moments of special awareness and recognition. Throughout our lives we have moments of deeper and deeper growth and formation. There may be moments of doubt, as though it's all too good to be true. But Jesus is always present, always available to us.

Third, conversion. Jesus sought the healed man out after his expulsion from the temple.

> Jesus...said, "Do you believe in the Son of Man?" He answered and said, "Who is he, sir, that I may believe in him?" Jesus said to him, "You have seen him and the one speaking with you is he." He said, "I do believe, Lord," and he worshiped him. (John 9:35–38)

At this point the man truly experienced Christ's presence and his love. This is what all people seek—to know Jesus Christ and the Father who sent him (see John 6:29). This is a personal knowledge. It is a relationship, an opportunity to grow in intimacy with the Creator and Redeemer.

CHOOSING TO BE A CHRISTIAN

As you prepare to evangelize, your own relationship with Jesus is crucial. You want to be what he calls you to be—to be like him, to be a Christian.

What is it like to be a Christian? What happens to me? How do I live, speak, and act?

No one wants to sound silly or become something like a religious nut. If you choose to be a Christian, you will live, speak, and act as Christ does—but in your own way. You are who you are. You are special as you are. At the same time you are growing into a better, happier, and more peaceful you.

I had a life-changing experience back in 1976.

I am a cradle Catholic, and I found my way into Catholic newspaper work, writing and selling some advertising. I loved the Church and believed in everything the Church taught. I knew God was real. But he seemed distant, almost inaccessible. I did not have a healthy fear of him; I was actually a bit terrified.

I dove into life with great energy; my attitude was "Damn the torpedoes, full speed ahead!"

But I always felt inadequate. There was worry and anxiety over this or that real or imagined problem. I even tried alcohol as a way of resolving my difficulties.

I had a poor prayer life. Oh, I went to Mass and said some prayers, but I proudly proclaimed, "My life and my work in the Church are my prayer." Would that it had been so!

Then, on October 31, 1976, I experienced God's love in a deep and personal way. Someone who has become a dear friend over the years prayed with me—Sr. Briege McKenna, o.s.c., known far and wide as the "healing nun." Her prayer—and my "at-last" decision to let the Lord into my life—was the beginning of a great, exciting adventure into a world filled with beauty, wonder, and joy in spite of its many scars and problems.

You see, before this experience I knew about God and the teachings of the Church. Suddenly I knew the Lord. I knew that he loved me personally, that I could do nothing that could make him stop loving me.

Living *in Jesus* became the awesome invitation—an invitation I wanted to accept, *had* to accept, and did accept. Now I no longer merely acquiesce to what the Church teaches; I embrace it. The Scriptures are alive, and they speak to me in my everyday situations.

The decision to be a Christian is a very serious one with eternal ramifications. My friend Fr. David Knight, a priest of the Memphis diocese, puts it clearly in his book *Reaching Jesus*.

...We have to be deeply convinced that Jesus Christ is not an option, that seeking total relationship with him is not an "extra." Only a relationship with Jesus can save us from veering off into destructiveness, distortion, mediocrity and meaninglessness.

If we think the choice before us is just a choice to be more rather than less—more Christian, more holy, more religious, more devout—we don't understand the question. It is not a question of more or less; it is a question of either-or.[5]

In the Eucharistic Prayer at Mass, the priest says, "Through him, and with him, and in him, O God, almighty Father, in the unity of the Holy Spirit, all glory and honor is yours, for ever and ever." This expresses a triple-faceted movement into the heart of God, who is Father, Son, and Holy Spirit.

Now that I experience Jesus's presence in my life, I want to live not only *for* him but *in* him. Living *in him* gives me a share in his wisdom, love, and power—to know as he knows, to love as he loves, to give my life to and for the kingdom of God.

FOR REFLECTION

- What is your recollection of the first time you became aware of Jesus?
- Did you develop a productive curiosity about him and about what he might mean in your life?
- Do you have any additional insights from the story of the blind man?

CHAPTER THREE

Knowing Jesus

Jesus said to him, "Have I been with you so long a time and you still do not know me, Philip? Whoever has seen me has seen the Father. How can you say, 'Show us the Father'?"

—John 14:9

How do we respond to the great gift of salvation? How do we grow in holiness and become the kind of Christians whom Jesus wants us to be and the Church needs us to be?

To know the Lord and to follow him faithfully requires effort. To achieve this goal, we commit ourselves to prayer, Scripture, worship, and life in community with our fellow Catholics and religious leaders. Such a commitment involves time, reflection, and formation on our part as individual disciples who are part of the worshiping and ministering Church.

Let's reflect on prayer, Scripture, worship, and community.

PRAYER

Step back a bit and examine your understanding of prayer. Does your way of praying help you to sense God's presence? Do formal prayers, such as the Our Father and the Hail Mary, involve your mind, heart, and soul, or are they just so much rote with a lot of distractions? Do you pray spontaneously? Do you have conversations with God?

Formal prayer is good. But when you pray formal prayers, think about what you are saying and reflect on the words and their meaning. St. Augustine said that there is no prayer on earth that cannot be found in the Lord's Prayer.[6] So let's take a moment to consider it.

Our Father,...

How dare I call you Father—you who are without beginning or end, totally holy, love itself? For I am a mere mortal, weak and sinful. Yes, I dare—because Jesus has taught me to so address you. Even more, he called you *Abba*, that endearing name we know as *Daddy*.

You are my Father: You give me life; you hold me in being and call me, in Jesus, to eternal life. Yes, Father! Abba!

who art in heaven,...

Lord, I long to be with you in heaven. My heart and soul yearn for the everlasting glory, peace, and joy of heaven.

But to arrive at this blessed state, I must first die. I am afraid to die. My entire being rebels at the thought of total dissolution. And yet I know I will not ever cease to exist. You created me to live forever. And so I shall.

And while I live on this earth, I live in you—and you are heaven: You are glory and peace and joy. You are love. At this moment and at every moment when I live in you, I already experience heaven.

hallowed be thy name.

When I say "God" or "Lord," even when I say "Jesus," I speak a mystery I cannot fathom, of a being I can never fully know or comprehend. Yet, my Lord and God, you call me your child, your disciple. I dare to call you by name because you, in great love and benevolence, have called me into an unimaginable intimacy. So I name you "Lord," "God," and "Father" and seek ever more to understand your holiness, majesty, mercy, and justice.

Thy kingdom come, thy will be done, on earth as it is in heaven.
In your will, Lord Father, is all that is good. Living as you want me to live is where your kingdom begins in and for me. If I accept Jesus as my own personal Savior—as the Way, the Truth, and the Life—I begin to get a glimpse of what is at last to come.

Help me, Lord, to make heaven "happen" now in my own life, so others may see your goodness. Help me to live a life so full of grace and obedience to you that I can become a beacon of hope, a sign of peace, and a gift of love to everyone in my life—to help heal this world so torn by hatred, greed, and disbelief.

Give us this day our daily bread,...
Your Word, O God, nourishes my mind and soul and brings light into the darkness of my understanding. Your gift of Jesus in the Most Holy Eucharist is the most precious of all food. When I receive him, Father, I receive your mercy and forgiveness, your holiness and your call to live a life of faith. You fill me so I may become "food" for others by the witness of my life of faith.

Help me, Most Holy Trinity, to share with others the truth and glory of this Eucharist, this holy nourishment you so generously offer to all who believe and come to it in faith. And, Father, I thank you for all you give me and my loved ones—food, shelter, clothing, medical care, and all other things necessary for our life on earth.

... and forgive us our trespasses, as we forgive those who trespass against us, ...
Lord Jesus, you saved us by your death. You chose the cross so we could begin to understand the love that you, the Father, and the Holy Spirit

have for us. Your death could have been enough for our redemption, but you spoke those immortal words that both teach us and free us from fear and despair: "Father, forgive them, they know not what they do" (Luke 23:34).

Jesus, you gave us a sobering truth. We will be forgiven only if we forgive. How can that be? Could it be that forgiveness is the greatest and irrefutable sign of love? If I refuse to forgive, I do not love as you love, as you commanded me to love: "Love one another as I love you" (John 15:12).

... and lead us not into temptation, but deliver us from evil.
Surely, Lord, you do not *lead* us into spiritual danger. But it comes. You permit it. It's part of the price we pay for original sin, and it's the battlefield on which our love for you is so often sorely tested. Satan hates you and us—and he is always trying to make us love ourselves and things more than we love you.

Lord, you stand ready to help us choose grace over sin. I know how strong temptations can be. I have sinned over and over again—failed to love my enemies, to help others when I could have, to keep my mind free of inane distractions and even potentially disastrous ones. So, Father, through the precious blood of Jesus, save me. Deliver me from sin because of your love.

Save us all, Lord; save us all!

Amen!
So be it! Amen!

Try this type of reflection with other formal prayers of the Church—the Hail Mary and the Acts of Faith, Hope, Charity, and Contrition. Don't forget the importance of the Apostles' Creed and the Nicene Creed.

TALKING TO GOD

You can also pray spontaneously, in your own words. Have a conversation with God. Talk to him as you would a friend—for he is the best friend you will ever have.

Personal, spontaneous prayer helps you develop honesty with God. It enables you to let off steam as well as praise God. The secret is to be yourself. God knows you, and you cannot shock him. According to one frequently told anecdote, St. Teresa of Avila actually complained to God one day after she fell in the mud: "If this is how you treat your friends, it's no wonder you have so few."

God knows all your regrets, hopes, secrets, and sins. And he loves you not in spite of all that but simply because he loves you. His love is like a mother's love, which never stops no matter how her child disappoints her. As God said through the prophet Isaiah:

> Can a mother forget her infant,
>> be without tenderness for the child of her womb?
> Even should she forget,
>> I will never forget you.
> See, upon the palms of my hands I have written your name.
> (Isaiah 49:15–16)

Don't forget to listen in prayer. God speaks to you in those precious moments when you put aside all your druthers and needs, when you stop telling God how to answer your prayers. When you listen calmly and intently to God's word for you, you will discover that peace that you once thought beyond your reach. You will come to realize just how close God is to you and how intimately he wants to relate to you.

Permit a personal example. In 1959, I was invited to work full-time for the Catholic paper in the diocese of Lafayette, Louisiana. I had no experience in journalism. In Texas, when Peg and I were first married, I drove a garbage truck, built fences, and read and repaired water meters. In Louisiana, I worked with the highway department as an engineer's aide supervising roadway construction.

Now, concerning this new job—with a wife, three children, and another on the way—I had a lot to think about. Just about everyone—uncles, aunts, friends, and even our pastor—discouraged me from taking it. But years before I had made a vow to Our Lady that if our one-year-old son survived a serious illness, I would return to the sacraments and someday, if God wanted, would work for the Church. My son survived, and here I was.

I didn't really understand the wonder and gift of prayer, but one day I knelt at the foot of our bed, praying the rosary. I kept asking God, "Do I or don't I?" At one point, when I asked, "Do I?" I was filled with a great peace. I knew I was going to work in Catholic journalism. That was in 1959, and I'm still at it.

God is your Creator, Redeemer, and advocate. Be at home with him, for he lives in you. God wants you to be so much a part of him that you and he can live in fellowship. That's how it was before Adam and Eve sinned, when they would be with God in the cool of the evening (see Genesis 3:8). God wants to restore that intimacy with you.

Pray every day—giving God quality time, not a moment here and there, sandwiched between e-mails and phone calls and work and play. Have a daily date with God, a time that is sacred to you and him. Let nothing except a real emergency deny you that time with God.

SCRIPTURE

Your next avenue of growth is praying and living the Scriptures.

When a loved one is away, you need to stay in touch. You need to say, "I love you," and you need to hear, "I love you." You do so by writing letters and e-mails, texting, and making phone calls. God has communicated his saving love for us through holy Scripture—through the Old and New Testaments. When we reflect on what God has said over the millennia since creation, we become aware of the horror of sin and are drawn more deeply into the mystery of gratuitous salvation. This enables us to communicate with God more easily in prayer.

Read and meditate on Scripture daily. I guarantee that as you make Scripture a priority in your life, you will grow to love God and his word. Ask God to open your mind and heart to whatever he wants to tell you at that particular moment. Read slowly, savoring the words, the descriptions of people and places. Use the imagination God has given you.

Say you want to read about the birth of Jesus (see Luke 1—2). *Read* it as you would any other story—for it is a story, a divinely inspired one.

Now stop a minute and *think* of what impressed or inspired you. Was it the angel coming to Mary? Was it the birth of Jesus in a stable? Whatever part of the story grabbed your imagination, stay with it for a while.

Reread the Scripture—but only a small section at a time. Be present to the drama unfolding before you in God's love story. Pope John Paul II taught that everything Jesus did on earth is eternally present to the Father; you, he said, can enter into the reality of that historical moment and live it in contemporary time by use of your will, imagination, and desire.

So, for example, be present to Mary and Gabriel at the Annunciation. Note Mary's humility and hesitancy—and her willingness to do what God wanted her to do. Stand in awe at the realization that the Holy Spirit of God has placed the Son of God in her womb.

Now think: *What does this mean for me?* How do I conceive Jesus in my heart, mind, and soul? How do I become more open to God's will, to the presence and action of the Holy Spirit in my life? Think prayerfully and gratefully of the times God has touched you and given you an awareness of his presence in your life.

This exercise can be a source of great spiritual growth as you read any section of the Bible. Holy Scripture, both the Old Testament and the New Testament, has pulled me closer to God. It has spoken to me in special and inspiring ways.

When God healed me of alcoholism, I discovered this message confirming his gift.

> I waited, waited for the LORD,
>> who bent down and heard my cry,
> Drew me out of the pit of destruction,
>> out of the mud of the swamp,
> Set my feet upon rock,
>> steadied my steps,
> And he put a new song in my mouth,
>> a hymn to our God;
> Many shall look on in awe
>> and they shall trust in the LORD. (Psalm 40:1–4)

This Scripture passage found a home in my heart. Sharing it in the context of God's merciful healing has led others to embrace sobriety.

Scripture is alive—and you can live it today. Ask the Holy Spirit to enlighten you as you read and reflect on God's Holy Word.

WORSHIP

There is no greater worship than the Mass, where we witness the salvation won for us by the Lord Jesus Christ. In all the sacraments we encounter God in a deeply personal way. In the Eucharist we also celebrate our unity with our fellow Christians.

To better appreciate and celebrate the Mass, you must realize that you are not merely *remembering* what Jesus did two thousand years ago; *you are living it with him.* As Pope John Paul II said, everything Jesus did on earth is an eternal reality. When we come to worship, the liturgy makes present in time what is always before the Father in eternity.

Pay attention during the liturgy. Follow closely the spiritual journey of the Mass. In the readings we have the dynamic, ever alive history of salvation. We can hear God speaking to us and be drawn into the journey with all the prophets and saints.

In the Eucharistic Prayer the bread and wine become Jesus Christ—his Body, Blood, Soul, and Divinity. We actually sit with Jesus in the Upper Room, stand at the foot of the cross, and walk with Mary Magdalene to discover an empty tomb and the Risen Lord himself. And the Lord Jesus calls us forth to receive him; we receive him in real time but with those first disciples at the first Mass in the Upper Room. That's the glory of the Mass, of our Catholic faith.

How could Mass ever be boring? There we have both God's word and the Eucharist. If either were omitted, worship would be impoverished. If you have decided to be a Christian, to follow Jesus Christ, to give his love and earthly presence in your own flesh and spirit, you will embrace the Mass with gratitude and a passionate desire to become one with God.

The Mass and the sacraments are the lifeblood of the Church, God's guarantee that he loves us and saves us. Through the power of the sacraments our ordinary lives become extraordinary as we become ever more deeply united to God and his people.

THE FAITH COMMUNITY

Since we married, Peg and I have belonged to seven different parishes. In each one there were certain strengths that fostered faith and a sense of belonging. By far St. Mary Magdalen, our present parish, has provided us with the best "home" and extended family.

We tend to measure the success of a parish by how well our own needs are met, including our need for opportunities to grow spiritually as individuals and as a Catholic community of faith. A short list of such opportunities includes meaningful liturgies, with special emphasis on instructive and inspiring preaching and a talented and faith-filled choir, and ongoing religious education and formation for persons of all ages, married and single, widowed and divorced, rich and poor.

In our parish, love is such a bonding force that it is virtually impossible to have silence in the body of the church before Mass. People greet and hug one another, share information about what's on the agenda for this ministry or that meeting, find out who's sick and who's dying. I'm reminded of what Jesus said: If you try to silence these folks, the very stones will cry out! (see Luke 19:40). It's a family affair. But when Mass begins the only sound is the voices of all these brothers and sisters raised in prayer, praise, and song.

In your decision to be a Christian, you have chosen to be part of the Church, the New Jerusalem, the pilgrim people, the body of Christ. There are no Lone Ranger Christians. Even the hermits of old were required to come back into the monastery community on a regular basis. It is in community, at Sunday worship, that we are instructed and nourished by God's word and the Eucharist. Together we bring all that we are—all our hopes and regrets, our joys in all that is good, our sorrow for sin, and our gratitude for the blessings of our earthly life. Together we permit God to absorb us into himself and to blend us into one joyful harmony of praise and fellowship. In a parish we grow as Church—the Church of Catholic Christians who follow Jesus and do what he wants us to do.

To be an effective Catholic lay evangelist, you must be strongly situated in the body of Christ. You must be part of the whole, living vibrantly the life of grace in communion with the Church. You add to and take from the strength of the Church.

To grow closer to the Lord and to others in your parish, see if you can join a Bible study group, a rosary group, or a parish ministry, such as one dedicated to serving the sick or the bereaved. Try to associate with people who display serenity, peace, and spiritual energy for good.

TAKE ANOTHER LOOK

Let's take a minute to review the steps toward spiritual maturity.

Make prayer a priority. We want to be healed and fueled by prayer. To pray well and maturely, schedule a special, nonnegotiable daily appointment with God. It is a time to praise him, thank him, and listen to him—to be open to what God wants to whisper into the depths of your heart and soul.

Make Scripture a part of your daily life. Read your Bible. You may want to join a responsible Bible study group or use a popular aid such as *Magnificat, God's Word Today,* or *Shorter Christian Prayer.* The latter is part of the Liturgy of the Hours, the prayer of the Church. The congregation in our parish prays Morning Prayer from this book at the beginning of the 8:30 AM weekday Mass.

Attend Sunday Mass and even daily Mass when possible. There is no better way to gain strength and grace than through the Eucharist. When you worship at Mass with your brothers and sisters, you are experiencing intimacy with God and with all the saints living here and in heaven. Reflect on the Mass—see how you are called into intimacy with Christ as he suffers, dies, and rises again.

You also encounter the Lord in a special and beneficial way when you pray before the Blessed Sacrament. There you can be present to the risen, glorified, and alive Jesus. He waits in that tabernacle for you. He desires to bless you, enlighten you, and form you into his very image.

Remember you are a member of the Church, the Body of Christ. That's your locus in all facets of your Christian life. It is in and through the Church that you are called to the life of grace, to the sacraments, to the table of the Lord, and to the Word of the Lord.

If you devote yourself to these areas of growth, you can honestly say, "I am a Christian."

For Reflection

- What steps can you take to improve your prayer life?
- How can you make Scripture a more meaningful part of each day?
- When you are at Mass, try to experience yourself as present, with all the others, at the foot of the cross. What are you thinking and feeling?

CHAPTER FOUR

Called
to
Be
a
Disciple

I give you a new commandment: love one another. As I have
loved you, so you also should love one another. This is how all
will know that you are my disciples, if you have love for one
another.

—John 13:34–35

In rediscovering [Christ's] love day by day, the missionary
commitment of believers attains force and vigour that can
never fade away. Faith…makes us fruitful, because it expands
our hearts in hope and enables us to bear life-giving witness:
indeed, it opens the hearts and minds of those who listen to
respond to the Lord's invitation to adhere to his word and
become his disciples.

—Benedict XVI, *Porta Fidei*, 7

You can intellectually assent to the humanity and divinity of
Christ and to his miracles. You can pray every day and never
miss Sunday Mass. You can be kind to people. You can do all
that and yet still fall short of being a committed disciple.

What does it mean, then, to be a disciple of Jesus Christ? It means you do what Jesus did: You love as he loved. You reach out to the sick, the disenfranchised, and the poor—both the spiritually and materially poor. You bring them the Good News.

Recall how Jesus sent out the twelve (see Luke 9:1–6). He "gave them power and authority over all demons and to cure diseases, and he sent them to proclaim the kingdom of God and to heal." The twelve had not yet been "ordained." Jesus had not yet laid hands on them to make them leaders of the Church. They were still laypeople, and he sent them to do what he did—to preach and to heal.

At another time Jesus sent out seventy-two disciples to cities he was to visit, to help prepare the way for his ministry (see Luke 10:1–12). They were to announce his coming. This is part of the Lord's ministry of evangelization, to which he calls his disciples.

CALLED TO CARRY THE CROSS

Jesus was clear that his ministry was not all glory, power, and joy. He spoke of the stress and opposition we will encounter in our evangelistic mission. "He said to all, 'If anyone wishes to come after me, he must deny himself and take up his cross daily and follow me'" (Luke 9:23).

Just what is your cross?

You choose to live a moral life. You honor and cherish commitments in your marriage, your friendships, and your work. Sometimes it is hard to honor commitments, especially when it involves forgiving injuries and working when you feel ready to drop. This pain can be your cross.

Jesus loved and lived for others. To be like Jesus, and to love as he loves, you must stand up for people who are put down or otherwise abused. You comfort the sick and pray for their healing. You bring hope to the hopeless. You treat your coworkers with respect and reverence. You do this regardless of the financial cost or the danger to your social standing. This again can be your cross.

You speak of God and your faith in him. You teach truth, and you may even call people to repentance. You are an active citizen, and you let no one silence your patriotic, faith-filled voice when you address social and government issues. This too can become a heavy cross.

You may be challenged by people as well as by the powers of darkness. At times you may be ridiculed or denied what is rightfully yours—whether a raise or a promotion.

A word of caution: You are not required to make a martyr of yourself.

I know a woman who had a strong sense of justice with respect to her coworkers, yet she was pugnacious and preachy. She never held a job very long; she either resigned or was terminated. You don't solve problems by preaching, and you surely don't call people into the kingdom if your attitude is one of condemnation. It takes both patience and gentleness to correct wrongs in the name of Christ.

Bill Lawless, now a practicing attorney, had the opportunity to do just that many years ago. He was at work when two men who had previously been friendly began looking at him in a rather strange way. He asked them what was wrong. They said they didn't "want to get him mad."

He said, "If something's wrong and you don't tell me, I will be mad."

The men told Bill that their preacher the past Sunday had said that Catholics were in allegiance with the pope, who planned to take over the United States. The pastor told his congregation that local Catholics were storing arms and ammunition in the basement of their church.

Bill asked the two men to take a little ride with him. He took them to his parish church. "Now," he said, "I want you to go in there and open every door and every drawer to see if there are any weapons." They objected. He insisted.

Bill followed the men into the church. After their search he asked them, "Did you find any weapons or ammunition?"

"No, we did not."

"Now," Bill said, "follow me outside." He told them to look under the church. "Do you see a basement?"

"No, there is no basement." The church was on sill blocks.

"So there are no weapons in a basement in our church."

"No, there are not."

The next Sunday the two men stood up in their church and told the preacher he had lied to them. They told the congregation of their trip to the Catholic Church. That week the preacher was fired by the congregation.

Standing up for God and his Church is not always so dramatic. But let's not be tongue-tied when presented with criticism about our Catholic faith. Carry your cross with Jesus, who is always at your side.

BECOMING LIKE JESUS

We must strive for a level of spiritual maturity at which we are so "one with Jesus" that we cannot imagine any other way of life. His mind and will become the motivation for all our thoughts and actions. We can say with St. Paul, "I have been crucified with Christ; yet I live, no longer I, but Christ lives in me; insofar as I now live in the flesh, I live by faith in the Son of God who has loved me and given himself up for me" (Galatians 2:19–20).

It is in this, the living *in* Christ, the Son of God, that we experience resurrection in the present life. Like a woman who forgets her pain once her baby is delivered and placed in her arms, our crosses are no longer burdens (see John 16:21). They become joy—for we have suffered with Christ, died to self for love of him and others, and now experience the wonder of full conversion and intimacy with God.

A disciple wants to be like Jesus. What does that mean? Two significant traits come to mind: his unconditional love and his obedience to his Father.

First, so great was his love that Jesus never tired of helping people—feeding the hungry, curing the sick, and preaching the Good News. It is to this ministry that we, disciples of Jesus Christ, are called. With him and in his Spirit, even when we are fatigued and feel that all our efforts are in vain, we go on as he did. We find strength where he found his strength—in his Father and our Father. We imitate his way of praying, entering into the wonders of the Father's love. We give ourselves to the Father through Jesus.

Second, Jesus was obedient, even to the point of dying on the cross as a common criminal. That final and great obedience was built on a foundation of constant obedience to the Father. To fulfill his Father's desire to bring people into the kingdom, he responded in mercy when people misunderstood him or even betrayed him. When his chosen twelve got all confused and arrogant, seeking first place at his side, he led them to reflect on the cost of their faith in him (see Mark 10:35–41).

The Beatitudes are what I call the Jesus Pattern of Obedience:

Blessed are the poor in spirit,
    for theirs is the kingdom of heaven.
Blessed are they who mourn,
    for they will be comforted.
Blessed are the meek,
    for they will inherit the land.
Blessed are they who hunger and thirst for righteousness,
    for they will be satisfied.
Blessed are the merciful,
    for they will be shown mercy.

Blessed are the clean of heart,
for they will see God.
Blessed are the peacemakers,
for they will be called children of God.
Blessed are they who are persecuted for the sake of
righteousness,
for theirs is the kingdom of heaven.
Blessed are you when they insult you and persecute you and
utter every kind of evil against you because of me. Rejoice and
be glad, for your reward will be great in heaven.
(Matthew 5:3–12)

Jesus tells us to be meek, to be poor in spirit, and to suffer for his name's sake. We are to join him in feeling sorrow for the sad plight of sinners and for the despair of those with no hope. We are to thirst for justice. We are to be righteous (holy) in a world alienated and steeped in darkness.

If you want to be like Jesus, reflect on the Beatitudes. Reflect on them with Jesus as your model and guide. He calls you to be like him and in him—and he doesn't ask you to do the impossible. There is nothing he and you cannot achieve, handle, or overcome.

So Now What Do We Do?

Do you love God passionately? Do you trust him completely? Do you sizzle with his divine life? The Holy Spirit is ready to fill you with wisdom and courage.

It is time to step out in faith. Let God's love for you overflow into the lives of others. That's all it takes to begin to change lives and to change the world.

Perhaps you have heard the opinion that many Catholics have been "sacramentalized" but not evangelized. They have not yet experienced the blessing of knowing Jesus personally and intimately. They have not been introduced to the work and power of the Holy Spirit. These are the people who are the "sleeping giant" waiting to be awakened and put into mission in the world.

And there are other people in your life, who may or may not be Catholic, people you almost take for granted, people who need to see and hear your love for God—the teller at the bank, the stock clerk at the supermarket, and the receptionist in your doctor's office. If you truly love and respect them, you will want to show them God's love and invite them into the heart of God's Church.

> Since the entire People of God is a people which has been "sent,"…"the mission of proclaiming the word of God is the task of all of the disciples of Jesus Christ based on their Baptism." No believer in Christ can feel dispensed from this responsibility which comes from the fact of our sacramentally belonging to the Body of Christ. A consciousness of this must be revived in every family, parish, community, association and ecclesial movement. The Church, as a mystery of communion, is thus entirely missionary, and everyone, according to his or her proper state in life, is called to give an incisive contribution to the proclamation of Christ.
>
> —Benedict XVI, *Verbum Domini*, 94[7]

Some Catholics seem to cherish a false humility—the notion that "I am not worthy to be like Jesus," or "I could never do what Jesus did," or "I'm insignificant and don't presume that God is calling and sending me." That is not humility; it is a lie, perhaps even a subtle pride. It is almost a rejection of the gift of salvation and the work of the Holy Spirit in your life.

When God asks you to do something—like stepping out to evangelize—you may at first feel uncomfortable, even disbelieving. "Who, me, God?"

God may ask you to stretch a bit, as he did when he urged me into the Catholic press. He may want you to do what seems impossible. But if you are obedient to him, he will help you accomplish what he asks of you.

A consoling thought: Years ago the late Bishop Charles B. McLaughlin, of St. Petersburg, Florida, helped me get over some discouragement about our work at *The Florida Catholic*. He was a strong man who had served as a priest in North Carolina, where in those days Catholics were at best regarded with suspicion. He told me that God asks for effort and not success. You do what you have to do, he said, and leave the rest to God.

So shed false humility. Let's not be Catholic couch potatoes. Our goal is to spread the kingdom of God, not sit back and cheer others on.

Pray earnestly and with confidence. Ask Jesus to guide you through the Beatitudes—and make his way, his truth, and his life your very own.

Then do what Jesus did! Announce the kingdom of God. Perhaps this little prayer will help you along the way:

Jesus, I love you and trust you!

Help me to love you passionately and trust you completely! Amen!

FOR REFLECTION

- Are you called to be Jesus's disciple?
- What particular cross has Jesus asked you to carry?
- Do you believe that God can use you?

PART TWO

How
It
Is
Done

Incorporated into the Church by Baptism, the faithful...must profess before men the faith they have received from God through the Church. By the sacrament of Confirmation they are...more strictly obliged to spread the faith by word and deed....

...[S]o too the laity go forth as powerful proclaimers of a faith... when they courageously join to their profession of faith a life springing from faith. This evangelization, that is, this announcing of Christ by a living testimony as well as by the spoken word, takes on a specific quality and a special force in that it is carried out in the ordinary surroundings of the world....

Therefore, even when occupied by temporal affairs, the laity can, and must, do valuable work for the evangelization of the world.

—*Lumen Gentium,* 35

CHAPTER FIVE

Sharing Your Story

You are "a chosen race, a royal priesthood, a holy nation, a people of his own, so that you may announce the praises" of him who called you out of darkness into his wonderful light.

—1 Peter 2:9

C atholics who hesitate to share their faith do not necessarily lack the desire to do so. They may lack self-confidence. They most probably have misconceptions about what evangelization is and how to go about it.

Remember, evangelization is calling people to Jesus Christ. It is a process of sharing what God has done in our lives. It is not at first calling people into our sacramental life or teaching them the doctrines of the Church. That comes later, after the person has become interested in the hope and joy offered in a life of faith in Christ.

WORDLESS WITNESS

Take a Christian or a handful of Christians who, in the midst of their own community, show their capacity for understanding and acceptance, their sharing of life and destiny with other people, their solidarity with the efforts of all for whatever is noble and good. Let us suppose that, in addition, they radiate in an altogether simple and unaffected way their faith in values that go beyond current values, and their hope in something that is not seen and that one would not dare to imagine. Through this wordless witness these Christians stir up irresistible questions in the hearts of those who see how they live: Why are they like this? Why do they live in this way? What or who is it that inspires them? Why are they in our midst? Such a witness is already a silent proclamation of the Good News and a very powerful and effective one. Here we have an initial act of evangelization. The above questions will ask, whether they are people to whom Christ has never been proclaimed, or baptized people who do not practice, or people who live as nominal Christians but according to principles that are in no way Christian, or people who are seeking, and not without suffering, something or someone whom they sense but cannot name. Other questions will arise, deeper and more demanding ones, questions evoked by this witness which involve presence, sharing, solidarity, and which is an essential element, and generally the first one, in evangelization.

—Paul VI, *On Evangelization in the Modern World*, 21

Your own holiness is the best "gospel of freedom" you can offer. If you are holy and happy, people will know you are somehow different, and they will want what you have. Then you can tell them how God has worked in your life and how your faith community has helped you continue in your walk with the Lord in peace and harmony.

We may never know how our lived faith has affected someone. Ginny Seibert is blessed to see the fruit her witness has borne in her husband's life.

Jim Seibert, of the Orlando area, says that for twenty-five or thirty years he placed no value on a relationship with God. "The same independent spirit that influenced my earthly life had spilled over into my spiritual life. I was acting independent of God."

But, he says, when he met Ginny, "I saw a peace and calmness in her that wasn't in me. That awareness began the unraveling of my independence from God. Slowly I realized it was Ginny's Christian beliefs that were influencing her temperament. I began feeling an urgency to develop a relationship with God."

It wasn't an "overnight success" for Jim. "God gave me plenty of opportunities to 'test' him, but he always gave me a pass and changed my life. The drought is over. I've lost my independence from God."

Today Jim is involved in Catholic and interfaith Bible study groups. He also works closely with Hospice of the Comforter in Orlando, assisting people who are facing their own death or the death of a loved one.

ACTIONS LEAD TO WORDS

We tend to see the Church's social mission as efforts to give temporal aid to suffering men, women, and children here in our own country and throughout the world. To help these poor people is a sacred duty and a privilege as well; it is a command of Christ. But in any corporal work of mercy, there is an innate obligation to bring people the Good News of Jesus and the power of his Spirit in the Church.

Jack and Jean Canatsey have responded to Jesus's call to let their light shine before others in order to glorify the Father (see Matthew 5:16). Theirs is not a preaching ministry; it is a "doing" ministry. But when people ask them about their motivation, they speak of what the Lord has done for them through their Catholic faith.

In the early years of their marriage, the couple lived in Indiana. There they began visiting jails and prisons. They arrived in Florida in 1993 and eventually found themselves visiting a prison where someone close to them was serving time. There they met the families of prisoners, families that were confused, anxious, and often without the comfort of faith.

Jean and Jack developed relationships with these families and began meeting other people who had relatives in prison. Their efforts developed into a personal ministry, Families Ministering to Families. They have had some success in demonstrating God's love in friendly outreach.

One case rises to the surface. We'll call him Ralph.

Ralph's family—parents and siblings, uncles and aunts—had disowned him when he went to prison. When Ralph's father died, Jean and Jack tried to convince prison officials to let officers escort the man to his father's funeral. The officials denied the prisoner this privilege. The Canatseys told Ralph that they would go to the funeral in his place.

At the funeral Jean took a leap of faith and invited the entire family to the prison to visit Ralph. Jean smiles as she recalls, "Now, you just don't invite people to a federal prison without prior clearance—and you never are allowed more than two visitors at a time. But there we were, and we urged the prison officials to permit this visit, and they did.... Siblings, nephews, and nieces were allowed to visit Ralph."

Jack and Jean say that it was one of the most moving experiences of their lives. There were hugs and kisses and laughter—and all animosity was stripped away. That's what can happen when you step out in faith to help people in the name of Jesus.

Personal Sharing

Recently at a meeting of men involved in Scripture study, a man shared his story of how he had come to the Lord. His childhood had been rather dysfunctional and without religious involvement. He had many setbacks in life—and he admits to many wrong decisions. But, he said, "every time something bad happened to me, or I had gone wrong, I learned something." As he looks back on his life, he sees that all "dark clouds had a silver lining."

At age sixteen he fathered a child, quit school, and got a job to support his infant son. Eventually, married and still involved deeply with his son, he "realized something was missing in my life. I decided it was time to seek God. My life changed."

You could have heard a pin drop as this man was speaking. His conversational, almost shy presentation came from his heart. There was no dramatic effort to be convincing; the truth of his experience was obvious.

Your own personal experience with God's saving love and the stories of other people you know are the essential and foundational messages that will bring people to Christ. Tell others how you experienced conversion to Christ or how God's love saved your child or how his grace saw you through a terrible ordeal, such as the death of a loved one. People discover hope when they hear how God has helped you kick drug addiction or overcome resentment, anger, or fear.

Bob Olson, of Cromwell, Connecticut, has shared his story of conversion from being a nominal Christian to a dedicated Catholic who wants to help others discover the meaning of faith. His conversion was rather sudden—after many years in which he saw no need for God and was certain that God didn't need him.

One of Bob's daughters developed serious emotional problems. Things were tough, and he began to realize that "only God can handle something like this." In the course of his journey to God, Bob learned that 90 percent of people who face spiritual and emotional problems have not learned to forgive.

Ultimately Bob made a list of everyone who had ever hurt him and, one by one, forgave them. Then he made a list of everyone he had ever offended and asked God to heal whatever hurt he had caused. He chuckled, "This list was longer than the first one. I knew I had to apologize to these people and ask them to forgive me."

As occasions arose, he did just that. He began to sense a new peace in his life. People seemed to regard him more positively than before. When he was reconciled with God and the Church, he dedicated his life to helping others find peace and joy in Christ.

Bob's evangelistic energy mirrors the emphasis that Pope John Paul II placed on evangelizing or "reevangelizing" Catholics. He organizes laypeople to reach out to family members, friends, and coworkers who have left the Church. He especially loves to help people forgive and get free of resentment.

How to Organize Your Story

Your personal witness of God's presence and activity in your life is important. It will help people to seek God and to be open to his love and presence. So how do you tell your story?

First, it is important that evangelizers develop and embrace an attitude of "grateful repentance." God has been merciful to you: You felt unloved or discouraged or fearful—and you are perpetually grateful that Jesus did thus and so to lift you out of the mud. His love propels you to share his goodness and passionate love with others.

Second, continuously grow in your relationship with the Lord. I can't say this enough: If you are a committed disciple of Christ, you pray every day, attend Mass and receive the sacraments, live a moral life, and embrace all the truths the Church teaches. This keeps you in touch with the Lord and equips you for the mission of bringing people to the Father.

Third, think about how to tell your story. What was going on in your life before you came to know the Lord? You don't have to specify your sins—it's enough to say you were totally disoriented, unable to make sense out of life, in stressful family relationships, or what have you. What led you to ask Jesus into your life? Was it your spouse, a child, a pastor, a friend, a religious program on TV?

Fourth, describe how you experienced God's love. Was it a feeling of great warmth, a sudden sense of well-being, or new hope, peace, joy?

Fifth, examine how your life has changed. What has happened in your relationships? Is your prayer life changed? Are you truly a happier person? Do people acknowledge the change in you?

Finally, share your story conversationally. You are not preaching or teaching. You are giving humble and grateful witness to God's great action in your life. Be yourself. The "testimonies" I remember most from my sixty-plus years of listening to evangelists are those that were delivered simply and conversationally. Truth whispered is louder than shouts.

READY FOR THE TRAIN

Evangelization is rooted in good relationships—with friends, coworkers, and people you meet every day. We are not in the numbers game—"counting scalps," as someone once said. We want to help people discover the love and mercy of God right where they are.

Once Jim Seibert discovered God's love through his wife's witness, he was able to help four young men accept Jesus before they died. One was his own son Timmy, who died from AIDS. Later there was Butch, who also had AIDS. The young man's father asked Jim to talk to Butch and see if he could move him in his last days to accept the Lord.

"I visited Butch, and the first thing out of his mouth was, 'I don't want any Jesus stuff.' I said I understood but asked if I could open and close my visit with a prayer. He looked at me for what seemed like a minute and said, 'OK.'

"Butch and I met eight to ten times over the next eight weeks. During that time I slipped a little 'Jesus stuff' into the conversation. In every visit Butch talked about his 'train coming into the station'—meaning he was going to die."

Then one day Butch asked Jim, "What do you know about AIDS?"

Jim told him about his son Timmy. "From that time on," said Jim, "it was like we were on an even playing field."

The next visit brought another big question: "What do you think about gay men?"

Jim answered, "Butch, what do you want me to think? God loves all of us and maybe you a little more." Butch liked that response.

Then Jim said, "Butch, when the train pulls in, you can go left or right. If you go left there will be total darkness. If you go right you will see a bright light with a hand out to greet you. God is waiting there for you."

One morning the light on Jim's answering machine was flashing. Butch was dying. Jim went to the hospital and said, "Butch, your train is coming into the station."

Before Butch breathed his last breath, he wanted to hear that "Jesus stuff" and accept Christ into his life. "I kissed him on the forehead and said a prayer with him. Butch died an hour later."

Announcing the Kingdom

St. Paul instructed Bishop Timothy: "Proclaim the word; be persistent whether it is convenient or inconvenient" (2 Timothy 4:2). Of course, laypeople do not have the ecclesial responsibility of bishops, priests, and deacons, but they do have the baptismal responsibility to witness to our faith. We must stand for the gospel and share God's love "whether it is convenient or inconvenient." We must do so gently and humbly, with kindness and respect for the dignity and conscience of the other person.

Mike was something of a skeptic when it came to religion. He saw no reason to believe in anything he could not see, and he could not see God.

Then Mike was caught in a crisis: He lost his job, and soon he was behind on his mortgage payments. He realized that his savings would carry him only about four more weeks. Mike was frantically looking for work and finding no openings anywhere.

One day, waiting along with several other people to see a job counselor, Mike noticed a man next to him, about his age, who was smiling and chatting with everyone. This man seemed to be immune to the anxiety and frustration Mike felt so deeply. Mike extended his hand, introduced himself, and asked, "What are you doing here?"

"My name is Paul, and I'm looking for work," the man replied. "I've been unemployed for seven months, and I need to find work right away. But nothing ever seems to open up for me."

Mike said, "For someone out of work for seven months, you seem so upbeat, even happy."

"I am."

"How can you be happy when everything is falling apart?"

Paul told Mike about his faith in Jesus Christ and his trust in God. "I know that my God loves me. I know that he cares for me and will help me work my way out of this. I need only to have faith—to trust him—and things will work out for the best."

"But," objected Mike, "nothing's happening. You haven't found a job."

"No, not yet," Paul replied, "but I am happy because I know God will come to my aid. I can face these difficulties with a peaceful and joyful heart," the sign that God was already at work in his life. "Because of Jesus, I know that God is my Father, and I can trust him as Jesus trusted him even as he hung on the cross."

Paul smiled compassionately at Mike and asked, "Why don't you try to see things through God's eyes? Why is he letting us go through these problems? How can he give you hope and peace of mind and heart?

"Mike, just tell the Lord that you want to love him and trust him. Put your entire life in his hands. He will never let you down."

Paul quoted what he said was his favorite Scripture in times of trouble:

> What will separate us from the love of Christ? Will anguish, or distress, or persecution, or famine, or nakedness, or peril, or the sword?… No, in all these things we conquer overwhelmingly through him who loved us. For I am convinced that neither death, nor life, nor angels, nor principalities, nor present things, nor future things, nor powers, nor height, nor depth, nor any other creature will be able to separate us from the love of God in Christ Jesus our Lord. (Romans 8:35, 37–39)

Mike had met a Christian. He saw in Paul a victory that nothing could take away—not poverty, joblessness, or any other problem!

Look for opportunities to share what God has done for you—how he has healed you or helped you make an important decision. Tell people how God has blessed you with a good family, a loving spouse, a roof over your head, and food on the table. (Strange, but many people seem to forget that God does indeed provide these basic and common blessings.)

Or perhaps your marriage and family life have been a rough, painful experience. In that event share how God has helped you through the tough times. Whom did he put in your life to help you? In what ways did he manifest his love for you? How did you get free of anger and resentment?

Pray each day for God to lead you to someone with whom you can share your faith. Be aware of the dignity and needs of people who serve you—the waiters and waitresses in restaurants, the clerk in the department store, the man or woman selling you a new set of tires, and even your doctor at your next visit. You'll brighten their workday, and you might open a door to some deeper sharing.

You can offer healing with compassion, becoming one in spirit with the sufferer. In a sense you "feel" the pain of the other—be it physical, emotional, or spiritual suffering. A compassionate relationship opens the suffering to God's healing power.

Often you can pray with the person. Thank God for the gift of this person. Praise him for his goodness. Ask God to let his healing love flow. Ask him to forgive both of you your sins and to strengthen you in your weaknesses. Pray for his will to be done and for the courage, faith, and strength to accept and to live in his will. Then encourage the person to trust God and to depend on him; to seek his will, his strength, and his grace, even and especially if you feel he delays in answering the prayer.

For Reflection

- Think about your personal faith story. What are the key elements you could share with others?
- With which of the lay evangelists do you most identify: Bob Olson, Jim Seibert, or Jack and Jean Canatsey? Why?
- Is there someone in your life who demonstrates the qualities of a lay Catholic evangelist?

CHAPTER SIX

Getting Started

Amen, amen, I say to you, whoever believes in me will do the works that I do, and will do greater ones than these, because I am going to the Father. And whatever you ask in my name, I will do, so that the Father may be glorified in the Son. If you ask anything of me in my name, I will do it.

—John 14:12–14

Some preparation will help you stand ready to share with people, as opportunities arise, what God has done in your life and what he wants to do in theirs.

WHAT COMES NATURALLY?

There are many ways to serve God and the kingdom. Consider first your natural gifts and abilities.

Are you a good caregiver? Maybe God is calling you to help a lonely and ill relative or neighbor. He may want you to train other people in this ministry.

Are you a great organizer? Maybe you can start a Bible study in your neighborhood or set up a retreat day for moms in your parish.

Do you have talents in music, art, or theater? Maybe you can help make liturgies more inspiring.

Are you a carpenter? Maybe you can help Habitat for Humanity or some other organization that builds and repairs homes for the poor.

Are you a computer whiz? Many older folks would appreciate help getting connected.

Do you have a gift for communication? You can use your gift to help train disciples for Christ. Maybe God is asking you to help people who have trouble expressing themselves or to help lectors in your parish develop better skills. God may want you to encourage teenagers to express their faith to other young people.

It is inspiring to see laypeople active in parish ministries and events. You too can find a service niche if you have not already done so—visiting the sick, teaching religious-education classes, cleaning the church, caring for the vestments, or cooking for parish events. As you engage in such ministries, remember to be a friend to everyone around you, to be ready to give support in crises, and to assist in daily needs. Most of all, God expects you to share your faith and to encourage others to live the Christian life.

Bob Olson, the dad who discovered the power of forgiveness, ministers in several different movements in the diocese of Norwich, including Missionaries of Holy Apostles at the Holy Apostles Seminary. He also works for the Hartford Archdiocesan Office of Charismatic Renewal. For more than twenty years he has been part of Presentation Ministries in Cincinnati, which promotes evangelization among the laity through small communities in several areas of the country.

Some Good Reads

Pope Paul VI's *On Evangelization in the Modern World* is available at the Vatican website, www.vatican.va. You'll want to read and reread it.

Mark it up. It's full of inspiration and practical direction and is perhaps the easiest reading ever to come out of Rome. It's short and to the point.

The documents from the Second Vatican Council are also important. Several are especially helpful for Catholic evangelizers: *Dogmatic Constitution on the Church*, *Decree on the Apostolate of the Laity*, *Decree on the Church's Missionary Activity*, and the *Pastoral Constitution on the Church in the Modern World*.

Now, a word of caution: These are rather lengthy and theological documents, for which you might appreciate some guidance. Perhaps your pastor or director of religious education can organize a series of classes on them. I suggest starting with the *Dogmatic Constitution on the Church* and the *Decree on the Apostolate of the Laity*. Also, Alan Schreck's *Vatican II: The Crisis and the Promise* is an easy-to-read summary of the teachings of the council and how we can apply them to the task of the Church.

The U.S. bishops' *Go and Make Disciples* is an inspiring and practical guide to help parishes become the evangelizing force Jesus calls the Church to be. It can help you determine where you are as a parish and what more you might do to serve the Church.

If you are not careful, you could end up studying and studying and never get around to evangelizing! The idea is to make study a continuous discipline in your discipleship. Try to read a bit every day.

WORK WITH YOUR PARISH

As I mentioned earlier, being part of a strong parish is a great benefit to personal growth. It also provides a place to start evangelizing.

Encourage your parish to schedule functions to reach out to alienated Catholics. Or you may want to have an evening of prayer for people who have fallen away from their faith. Your parish priests and deacons may be able to organize a series of homilies—for example, in Lent or Advent—encouraging parishioners to embrace the idea that faith is a precious treasure that needs to be shared.

Catholics need to be encouraged to accept evangelization as central to their life of faith. "Selling" evangelization to traditional Catholics is not always easy; it takes work to help people understand their responsibility.

In our own St. Mary Magdalen parish, we've had several programs over the years, including Come Home Sundays, to which we invited families who were not coming to Church, and a series of evening prayer sessions for inactive Catholics whose names were furnished by parishioners.

One year we included in our general intercessions during weekend Masses a prayer for a spirit of evangelization, based on Pope John XXIII's opening prayer to the Holy Spirit at the first session of Vatican Council II:

> Renew your wonders in this our day as of a second Pentecost; and grant that the Holy Church, united in one prayer, more fervent than before, around Mary the mother of Jesus, and under the leadership of Peter, may extend the kingdom of the divine Savior, a kingdom of truth, justice and peace. Amen.

After people have met Jesus and accepted him in their lives, we should introduce them to Catholic doctrine, discipline, and tradition. It isn't a question of either formal knowledge or a personal relationship with God in a faith community. Both are necessary.

Most Catholic parishes offer inquiry classes and the Rite of Christian Initiation of Adults (RCIA) for people interested in joining the Church. In the latter, people learn Church teaching based on Scripture and tradition. Catechists introduce them to the practice of prayer and the experience of Christian community.

People seeking entrance into the Church need to know what they are getting into. They need to be introduced, for example, to the belief in the Real Presence and the Mass as the re-presentation of the sacrifice on Calvary. They need to understand the importance and role of tradition and Scripture, the sacraments, the ministerial priesthood, the priesthood of the faithful, and legitimate authority in the governance of the Church. See appendix one for an outline of teachings based on the *Catechism*.

Many Catholic evangelizers become sponsors for the people to whom they have witnessed their faith. Often sponsors learn more about their own spirituality and faith as they attend classes with their candidates and answer their questions.

MAKE DISCIPLES

Back in the 1970s a new craze raced through businesses and parishes. It was called something like "reproduce-ability." You had to reproduce yourself—that is, line up someone to work along with you so that he or she might replace you someday.

A disciple of Christ is dedicated to bringing other people not only into the faith but also into active discipleship. We can never have too many disciples bearing witness to God's love, offering prayers for healing, comforting the bereaved, and announcing the kingdom.

If you want to become a better and more effective disciple and call others into discipleship, you may want to consider the following:

• Form a Bible study group with a view to helping men and women discover the thrill of being a disciple of Christ. Center on the

Gospels. Take advantage of the many Scripture-study DVDs offered by Catholic publishers.

- Take courses on Scripture, the sacraments, evangelization, and ministry in general. Focus your attention on ministry in the "real world"—where people live, work, and play—and in community efforts and projects.
- Get involved in religious education and formation of adults and children. Know what it takes to reach modern man and woman and child.
- Attend a Christ Renews His Parish retreat or a Cursillo, or join a prayer group—charismatic, rosary, or otherwise.
- Be with people who truly search the heart and mind of God. Form a group of friends who meet occasionally to share faith, prayer, life, love, and laughter.

FOR REFLECTION

- What are your gifts? How can you use them to spread the kingdom?
- Choose a document of the Church to study, and record any insights you gain about the faith.
- Pray that God will lead you to individuals whom he wants your life to touch. As you go through your day, are you aware of how he is answering your prayer?

CHAPTER SEVEN

Your Mission to Your Family

The gifts and the call of God are irrevocable.

—Romans 11:29

In any parish, every Sunday after Mass, as parents and grandparents gather to fellowship, one can hear sad discussions about teenagers and young adults who no longer feel any need for the Church. Also there are husbands and wives who attend Mass without their spouses. Somehow Frank or Mary became alienated from the Church, maybe even from God.

Many people feel hopelessly helpless as they face such situations. I wish I could offer you the proverbial silver bullet, but I can't. In our own family we face the same concerns. There is no "easy way out." Reconciliation—with family and Church—is generally a long process, often hampered by the tendency to blame someone or something for the trouble. But it's not a blame game. It's about growth in faith for the entire family.

Take heart. God never takes back his gifts. He never silences his call to peace of heart now and happiness for all eternity. Here are a few thoughts that may help you maintain balance and a sense of humor—and both are indispensable whenever you want to influence someone or settle a disagreement of any kind.

TEENS NEED CHRIST

A caution, born of my own personal experience, seems timely. Parents who are deeply involved in parish ministries and organizations must make that involvement second and subordinate to their ministry and mission to their own families, particularly when the children still live at home. As parents, we find that our baptismal priesthood and grace are given for the education, nurturing, and formation of our children, God's gifts of love to us, the Church, and the world. "Parents are the ones who must create a family atmosphere animated by love and respect for God and man, in which the well-rounded personal and social education of children is fostered."[8]

That being said, let's focus on teens and then on young adults.

Remember, you were once right where they are. You were a teenager with new drives and emotions, confusions, and desires. Remember, too, the times you felt someone was trying to force you into something that was foreign to your own self-image.

The "good old days" gave your parents gray hair, and they probably let you know it. So develop a sense of compassion—a "suffering with" attitude. This will take the edge off your frustration and anger. Your teens will find you more understanding and supportive. This will greatly increase your positive influence on them.

Growing is painful. Physical and emotional growth can be painful; so is growing spiritually. It is a constant dying and rising. It begins with baptism and ends with your last breath. If you do a daily examination of conscience, you will be reminded of just how great and weak is the human mind and spirit. You will develop a sense of dependence on God, and this will be evident in the way you live as well as the way you speak.

The way you live is more important than any sage advice you might possibly give. Your own strong faith and love will serve you and your children in two ways: First, you will be at peace and less likely to lash out in frustration and anger; second, your children will more likely see your demeanor as a secure one. You must be a "safe place" for your children.

Parents committed to living their Catholic faith recognize where the truth line has to be drawn. They will not dilute Church teachings or the mandates of the gospel in an effort to entice their children to return to Mass and the sacraments. At the same time, they will make an effort to be what people in ministry call "pastoral." They will be gentle and listen intently and patiently when their children express frustration or show a spirit of rebellion.

I remember advice given to me by the late Msgr. J.G. Hanley from Canada. At a Catholic press convention many years ago, I was complaining to him about a headstrong child I couldn't bring into line. When I finally finished, he said, "Henry, why don't you give your children the same cordiality you give strangers?" Ouch!

God loves your family members more than you ever could. He, not you, created and redeemed them.

God gives you responsibility to lead your family according to the gospel of Christ, who is the way, the truth, and the life (see John 14:6). You may feel personal guilt, deserved or not, as you see your children draw away from the Church. Don't nurture that nagging or crushing guilt. Give yourself credit for doing as well as you could, what you thought was best. You acted on what you understood and experienced as you struggled to rear your children.

Both you and your family members learn from past mistakes. Thank God for the lessons learned, and beseech him to help you repair whatever alienation those mistakes might have caused.

Family meals are very important. There is something innately spiritual in eating together. Without food we die. As we eat together, we affirm life and our life together. We recognize our dependence on God, for our food comes from him—as does every breath we take.

The family meal is a good time to check on everyone's day—the good moments and the difficulties, perhaps with studies, at work, or with friends. Your sitting together at table is reminiscent of the greatest of all meals, the Last Supper and our celebration of that at Mass. *Eucharist* derives from a Greek word meaning "thanksgiving."

The atmosphere at the family meal will bring serenity and openness if the meal does not mimic the hectic rush of a fast-food joint. It is a time to shut out the world, to invite the peace of Christ into your life, and to relish the joy of being with people you love.

Work in love and with gentle determination. You may save your family members many years of estrangement from God, cynicism, and unhappiness. Sometimes it takes faith to remember that—but they have an innate dignity that must never be violated. If every member of the family is treated respectfully, the family will be stronger.

Even in disciplining youngsters, treat them with dignity. This can take the form of explaining why discipline is necessary and what you hope that discipline will accomplish. Discipline should never be punishment for the sake of coercion.

I remember the case of a young and immature father who thought severe physical punishment would make his children all behave the same way. He hoped to make them all be "good" so as to avoid parental embarrassment. It took years for the resulting emotional wounds to heal.

Your children were not all cut to the same pattern. They are different—from one another and from you. You can't expect them to embrace things in life as you do—sports, camping, family picnics, or books. They may or may not follow in your footsteps in profession, skills, or spiritual disciplines. They may or may not imitate the choice you have made for Christ and his Church. But surely you can expect them to mirror, at some time in their lives, your great love for them.

You can't force anyone, and especially your children, into God's arms. God doesn't force anyone, and if you try to, you'll only make matters worse. No one likes a bully. Only gentleness and love have any chance of calling your children back into the Church.

What jumps to mind here is the beatitude "Blessed are the meek, for they will inherit the land" (Matthew 5:5). Your gentleness and love will ultimately win the day.

Young Adults

Here there may be more baggage to sort out—and you can't do it independent of your loved ones. If they are alienated or apathetic adults, you will need to discover what is the root cause of their estrangement from the Church.

Was it inadequate religious education and formation? Perhaps you or other influential adults never spoke to them about the Lord, his love, and his Church. Many Catholics, as I've said before, have never experienced personally the warmth of God's love.

Were they offended by a leader in the Church—priest, deacon, religious, or lay leader? Some alienated Catholics I have encountered felt the Church never spoke to their needs. The only personal contact they remember or admit to was by phone or mail for this or that fund drive.

Some people have turned away from the Church because of specific teachings they find difficult to believe or embrace—for example, the prohibition of artificial birth control and cohabitation before marriage, the definition of marriage as the union of one man and one woman, and the discouragement of capital punishment.

In general, among these alienated adults there is an inadequate understanding of the nature of the Church and its sacraments. They lack the basic notion of God's calling to himself a people to be his own. Without this understanding, no Catholic can develop a deep and permanent sense of belonging and so cannot develop a desire to be with the Church.

Some alienated Catholics have joined other churches, perhaps a nondenominational congregation. These churches often appeal to alienated Catholics because they are entertaining in a way: They have great music and "make you feel good." Other former Catholics claim that in their new church they have been able to grow into a deep and personal relationship with Jesus Christ.

For us rock-solid Catholics with loved ones leaving our Church, hope reigns supreme: "Maybe someday they will come back home." But will they come home if we don't find a way to help them experience the presence of the Lord and his love in our midst?

Among those who do come home, a longing for the Eucharist is a major reason. This, I think, is a key to keep Catholics home and bring others back. The Eucharist is the center and force of our faith. Are we convinced of that?

Consider these suggestions for reaching out to alienated adult family members:

Recapture the sense of wonder in ordinary, everyday experiences. Bonding with loved ones is an ongoing process. An impromptu invitation to an adult child for a casual get-together can show your desire to spend time with him or her. Invite your young adult to share a movie, local sports event, or shopping excursion. Or go out together for a delightful chocolate shake or cup of coffee. Help your young adult experience the joy of living. Or maybe you need to learn it from the young adult!

Sharing a ball game or lunch may not seem very spiritual. Yet such ordinary moments can effect positive relationships in your family. St. Thomas Aquinas, one of the greatest spiritual writers in the history of the Church, reminds us that "grace builds on nature." What can be more natural than to enjoy time with someone you love—no agenda, no cajoling or preaching, just enjoying good stuff together?

You can't live the life of faith outside your own skin. Your family cannot be a Christian family outside the nitty-gritty of everyday living. So sit with your loved one as the world zooms by, and let your mutual love and respect form a comfort zone in the middle of all that hustle and bustle. Stay connected. Such joyful moments can cement your relationship as parent and adult child.

Don't let your own need for spiritual success lead you to become a constant nag. Harping on that baby who has not yet been baptized, for example, can lead to resentment. I've baptized many children in my twenty-five years of diaconal service. It is easy to spot the parents who truly want their children baptized and those who were cajoled into it by well-meaning grandparents.

Share your own early struggles with your adult children. Tell them how God acted in your life when you were their age. Did you have problems with obedience, smoking, drinking, or perhaps even drugs? If so, you know what it feels like to struggle with addiction and with rules that seem to work against freedom or personal preference. I've seen, in the eyes of family members and others, the welcome realization that "well, you do have some idea of what it's like." As in the case of younger children, parents and grandparents will recognize where the truth line has to be drawn.

Pray. Just as you ask God to help you find someone who needs your witness of faith, ask God to give you the opportunity and the wisdom you need to help adults and young people in your family. Pray in a collaborative way: You are not asking God to do the work for you; you are asking God to use you for his work. You are entering into the mind and heart of God. You are seeking his wisdom.

Here's a good prayer for your children:

> We do not cease praying for you and asking that you may be filled with the knowledge of his will through all spiritual wisdom and understanding to live in a manner worthy of the Lord, so as to be fully pleasing, in every good work bearing fruit and growing in the knowledge of God, strengthened with every power, in accord with his glorious might, for all endurance and patience, with joy, giving thanks to the Father, who has made you fit to share in the inheritance of the holy ones in light. He delivered us from the power of darkness and transferred us to the kingdom of his beloved Son, in whom we have redemption, the forgiveness of sins. (Colossians 1:9–14)

During Mass there are prayers for the needs of others, for peace in the world, and for political leaders of all nations. But the Lord wants to achieve much more in Catholic families through the Eucharistic sacrifice. We are to be a people who *become* Eucharist, the Body of Christ. The Eucharist magnifies in the Catholic spirit the call of

Christ to bring his saving life and death to the entire world. This sacred mission must be in the hearts of parents if they are to help their children discover their personal roles as disciples of Christ.

FOR REFLECTION

- What are some practical ways that you, as a parent or grandparent, can spend time with family this week?
- What can you share with your adult children about your own struggles that might encourage them in the faith?
- How vital is the Eucharist in your life? What are some ways it impacts you?

PART THREE

Let
the
Spirit
Act

When the Advocate comes whom I will send you from the Father, the Spirit of truth that proceeds from the Father, he will testify to me. And you also testify, because you have been with me from the beginning.

—John 15:26–27

CHAPTER EIGHT

The
Power
of
the
Spirit

A voice proclaims:

In the wilderness prepare the way of the LORD!

Make straight in the wasteland a highway for our God!

—Isaiah 40:3

We are all aware of the challenges facing us as evangelists today. Sexual immorality and materialism are but two of the trends that block people from receiving the word of God. And the process of conversion is no easy matter. We delight to hear a person take an initial step: "I want to know more about Jesus. I want peace in my life." But spiritual growth is a life-changing, challenging experience.

The good news is that God does not leave us helpless. He does not ask us to do the impossible. The Holy Spirit helps us relate to people who lack faith in God or, even having faith, feel overwhelmed by problems, suffering, and anxiety. The Holy Spirit will give understanding and wisdom to help people discover God's presence and healing power in their lives.

Jesus said:

> If you love me, you will keep my commandments. And I will ask the Father, and he will give you another Advocate to be with you always, the Spirit of truth, which the world cannot accept, because it neither sees nor knows it. But you know it, because it remains with you, and will be in you....
>
> ... The Advocate, the holy Spirit that the Father will send in my name—he will teach you everything and remind you of all that [I] told you. (John 14:15–17, 26)

The Holy Spirit—the Lord and Giver of Life, the Advocate, the Comforter, the Counselor, the Sanctifier—is the source of wisdom and power in all of Christian life. In baptism the Spirit brings the gift of holiness, the gift of divine life. And it is this same Spirit who provides us with special abilities, insights, and wisdom to do what Jesus did—to bring the Good News of God's love and salvation to others.

There are two kinds of spiritual gifts that the Holy Spirit imparts to the disciples of Jesus: the "transforming gifts," which make us Christians, and the "ministerial gifts," which empower us to serve the body of Christ. Here we will talk about the transforming gifts, and in the next chapter the ministerial gifts, or charisms.

GRACES AND GIFTS

When the Church speaks of grace, she speaks of sanctifying grace—the grace that makes us holy, which of course is the grace of the sacraments. The transforming gifts of the Spirit are part and parcel of sanctifying grace.

To do what Jesus did, we need the Holy Spirit and his gifts of transformation. In baptism we are filled with the divine life of God; our souls become conformed more closely to him. These gifts are strengthened in confirmation and nourished by penance and the Eucharist. And as these gifts make us like God, we become more successful and effective in all areas of our life—including evangelizing.

Let's consider the transforming gifts of the Spirit as described in Isaiah 11:2–3:

> The spirit of the LORD shall rest upon him:
>> a spirit of wisdom and of understanding,
>
> A spirit of counsel and of strength,
>> a spirit of knowledge and of fear of the LORD,
>> and his delight shall be the fear of the LORD.

Fear of the Lord. This gift of the Spirit lays the foundation for our growth in the love of God. To "fear" the Lord is not to live in terror of a distant, angry God but rather to stand in awe, to realize he and he alone controls all of creation and heaven too. He is all-powerful—and we are weak. He is all-holy—and we are poor sinners. He holds our very breath in his hands; he created us and holds us in existence.

Piety. In response to this God who loves us, the Spirit inspires and empowers us to worship him in love and service. When we experience God's love, we love him in return. That love for God must begin and end in worship and adoration. To worship God is to praise and thank him. To adore God is to stand in awe in his presence.

Fortitude. This is the gift of strength and perseverance—especially in that most critical area of our life, temptation to sin. Satan does not rest. He is constantly trying to trick us into trusting ourselves instead of God, into pursuing our own pleasures instead of the will of God. We receive the strength to stand fast in the face of persecution, ridicule, and even danger. This gift of fortitude also helps us overcome any fear or timidity that might discourage us from sharing our faith with others. It takes strength to do what Jesus did.

Counsel, knowledge, understanding, and wisdom. These gifts enable the disciple to discern correctly the difference between good and evil. God's word and his will find their home in us. Divine wisdom enlightens us to know that God is there for us always. We experience his inexhaustible passion for all people.

We can never capture or embrace the totality of God; he is simply "too big." And yet he embraces us and draws us into the depths of his love and wisdom. Here we can touch the greatness of God.

THE TRANSFORMING GIFTS AT WORK

The transforming gifts of the Spirit have practical consequences in people's lives. They produce what Paul collectively calls the "fruit of the Spirit." These are "love, joy, peace, patience, kindness, generosity, faithfulness, gentleness, self-control" (Galatians 5:22–23). These gifts affect our evangelizing. If you love, you can speak of love convincingly; if you are gentle, your words of a gentle God will be credible; if you have self-control, you will take time to discern the thoughts and needs of others; if you are generous, you will share your treasures—especially the treasure of your Catholic faith.

Consider the following examples:

Wisdom. With this gift the Holy Spirit helps us put on the mind of Christ, to see God as the ultimate good. This leads to greater union with God in mind and heart. As we allow wisdom to fuel our decisions in all areas of life—family, work, and finances—we experience profound joy.

Don Tauscher became one of the youngest successful businessmen in central Florida. By a sad turn of events, he lost his fortune and ended up owing tens of thousands of dollars. Committed to honesty and wanting to do what was right, he and his wife prayed for guidance. They decided they would repay every cent they owed—and over a period of years, they did.

But the story doesn't stop there. Don, through ecumenical contacts, discovered Crown Ministries, an evangelical, Bible-based, twelve-week process to help people get out and stay out of debt. He worked with Crown Ministries for some time and then made some adaptations to fit Catholic spirituality. At the time of Don's retirement, Crown Ministries was firmly established in more than forty dioceses around the nation. The ministry has changed hands and is now developing new, more massive appeal and outreach.

The gift of wisdom helped Don depend on God, solve his financial problem, and then help thousands of other people escape debt.

Fortitude. This gift strengthens us in times of temptation. We are faced with all kinds of temptation: We don't have to go far to be tempted sexually, and Satan's call to greed, pride, and hatred are incessant. We need the Spirit's gift of strength and courage to remain faithful to God and the Church. (For a magnificent, inspiring instruction, see *The Seven Deadly Sins,* a DVD featuring Fr. Robert Barron.)

Fortitude also helps us overcome certain personality weaknesses that limit our ability to share our faith and call others into the kingdom of God. I'm thinking of that timidity experienced by many Catholics when it comes to speaking of Jesus Christ and his gift of salvation. The Spirit's gift of strength and courage can make itself evident even in the depths of despair—such as in a prison.

"Tom" has been behind bars several times since he was seventeen years old. He is now several decades into a life sentence for murder. Tom has never denied his guilt. Initially shunned by everyone except an aged mother, he ultimately made peace with his only daughter.

A lay Catholic evangelist visited Tom, and the two became friends. Tom began to pray and read his Bible. He discovered God's love and has sought forgiveness.

Tom will never be paroled. He will die in prison. But he knows the "Lord of life." And the Holy Spirit has given him strength to live prison life in remarkable peace.

Piety. This is a gift of worship and love, a gift that enables the disciple to enter into deep communion with God.

"Dave" has a peace that is rooted in a marvelous and inspiring life of worship and reflection. He spends a lot of time in church praying before the Blessed Sacrament and at home meditating on Scripture. He listens to God and makes notes about the insights that come to him in prayer. His love of God grows as he worships—and his worship grows as he loves God.

Dave's serenity penetrates the hearts and minds of people around him. His worship of God enables him to see beyond surface concerns and bring to light the essence of a problem or a grace. God uses him to bring encouragement and spiritual consolation to others. The Holy Spirit always comes through.

FOR REFLECTION

- What transforming gifts of the Spirit have you experienced?
- Which areas of your life have been impacted by the Spirit's gifts?
- Which one of the transforming gifts are you most in need of?

CHAPTER NINE

The
Ministerial
Gifts
of
the
Spirit

Therefore, since we have this ministry through the mercy shown us, we are not discouraged. Rather, we have renounced shameful, hidden things; not acting deceitfully or falsifying the word of God, but by the open declaration of the truth we commend ourselves to everyone's conscience in the sight of God.

—2 Corinthians 4:1–2

There is more help from the Holy Spirit. He helps us witness to and serve other people. He helps us do what Jesus did through gifts that are given on an as-needed basis. These are sometimes called the charismatic gifts. I like to call them the Spirit's ministerial gifts—for they are used in ministry for the sake of others.

Among these ministerial gifts, which St. Paul lists in 1 Corinthians 12, are faith, healing, prophecy, the expression of wisdom, and the expression of knowledge (see 1 Corinthians 12:8–10). The Church teaches that we are to receive these graces in gratitude; they are important to the vitality of the Church and to the teaching, protection, and propagation of the faith. These special gifts are always authenticated by and exercised in charity and in communion with the Church's legitimate authority (see *CCC*, 798–801).

If you receive one or more of the ministerial gifts, they will be deeply rooted in your faith in God and at the same time outwardly dynamic—because you have that gift for the sake of your neighbor. Let's consider a few of these charismatic gifts in light of their importance in evangelization.

THE EXPRESSION OF KNOWLEDGE

The first time I experienced this charismatic gift was in 1976, when I went to Sr. Briege McKenna for prayer. I wanted to know God for real. I had been impressed by the stories of how God was working in the lives of people who had discovered the role of the Holy Spirit in the Christian life. When Sr. Briege prayed with me, the insights she had into my life were possible only through this ministerial gift of knowledge. This convinced me once and for all that God truly, really, without a doubt loved me and will always love me.

As Sr. Briege prayed, she mentioned two things she had no earthly way of knowing—as I had never told her. She said that my wife, Peg, and I should not worry about the child for whom we were praying fervently because of a tense life situation, and that I should not worry about a member of my family who had turned away from us and from God: "Jesus has his arm around him, and he's all right."

Another example of the gift of knowledge is this story about a lay catechist, "Bill," and a woman in a Sunday-morning convert class.

"Theresa" was seeking baptism in the Church. She spoke frequently of her past, and she seemed unable to move forward. One day, after she again expressed guilt over happenings of the past, Bill pulled her aside.

"Theresa, what is really going on?" Bill gently asked her. "Are you saying you can actually sin so much that God cannot forgive you? Is your past sin more powerful than God's love and forgiveness? You need to get over this. Trust God at his word. The past is the past. Read Psalm 103. There he tells you that he puts your sin as far away from you and him as the east is from the west. You need to move on."

In the group's retreat on Holy Saturday morning, Theresa said, "I realized that I was not letting God be God and that I was forgetting just how loving and merciful God is." That evening, at the Vigil Mass, when Theresa emerged from the waters of baptism, her eyes sparkled with joy, and her face was aglow with new life. She raised her hands toward heaven and, as she later explained, she told God, "I am yours."

This is why the Spirit gives the gift of knowledge—to help others realize once and for all that God loves them and that joy, peace, and happiness are what he wants for his people.

FAITH

This is not the faith that says, "Oh, yes, there is a God," or, "Oh, sure, Jesus died for us." Rather it is the gift to accomplish what we need to do, to meet the needs of someone even when we are surprised and unprepared. This is the faith of the evangelist, the faith that opens hearts and minds, the faith that will call people into God's kingdom.

A lay catechist was teaching on the need to forgive people who have hurt us. He mentioned that if we do not forgive, we cannot be forgiven—as is stated specifically in Matthew 6:14–15.

After the class a woman approached him in tears. She beat her fists on his chest, sobbing, "I can't forgive him! I can't forgive him!" Her ex-husband had abused her mentally, physically, and sexually.

The catechist asked, "Why can you not forgive him?"

She said, still crying, "Because if I forgive him, I'm saying I deserved what he did to me."

"I put my hands on her shoulders and looked her straight in the eye and said, 'Jesus did not deserve to die such a terrible death. But he forgave his executioners and us. His forgiving us did not mean he deserved what they did to him.'"

These words awoke a gift of faith in the woman and strengthened her will to do the right thing.

Two weeks later she approached the catechist. She was all smiles and seemed to be walking on air. "I did it," she said. "I forgave him."

HEALING

Certainly miraculous healings happen in our own day. I have witnessed such healings.

A tumor disappeared from the face of a seventy-two-year-old woman during a Mass in which the priest led us in a special prayer for healing.

A Florida woman was healed of alcoholism when her friend asked another person to pray for the healing. By the next morning the woman had lost all desire to drink, and she joined an AA group.

Two New Jersey men were healed of alcoholism—one when he heard an alcoholic give his witness about his own healing, and another when his wife asked a lay evangelist to pray with her for her husband.

Again in Florida, an elderly woman, through faith and prayer, was healed of cancer.

The most important part of healing prayer is always to seek God's will and to submit to his will. This might seem to be a cop-out or cover-up in case healing doesn't happen. Such is not the case. If God says no to a certain prayer request, it is only because he has something better in mind. The sufferer may learn more about God's love in pain than in comfort: Grandma may die after much prayer for her healing, but she will be in heaven pleading for you and your family.

There are doomsayers who claim that unanswered prayer is a sign of insufficient faith. If that's the case, Jesus in Gethsemane had insufficient faith. In fear and agony he asked his Father to spare him the torture and horror of the cross (see Luke 22:42). The Father's silence was a resounding *no*. Because Jesus accepted that *no* and embraced the Father's will, we are all redeemed.

PROPHECY

This gift from the Holy Spirit reveals God's will and light in present conditions and situations. It seems that it rarely predicts the future.

For example, at more than one prayer meeting, during periods of praise and worship, people have been moved to express a sentiment that came through prayer. In a time of great social stress, a woman said that God wanted his people to know that he was with them, that the burden they carried would be lifted and his love would be made manifest.

Another group of Christians were praying for God's intervention for a child who had been critically injured. A person said simply, "I sense the Lord saying this child will survive." And the child did.

This gift of prophecy also has huge social implications. When there are no laws to prohibit what is evil and harmful, Christian prophetic witness is imperative. There are no civil or criminal laws against publishing and consuming pornography (except where children are concerned). There are no human laws against adultery, cohabitation, and promiscuity. There are no laws forcing people to love and care for the poor and the helpless. Nor is the religious formation of children mandated by civil law—in fact, Congress and the courts seem hell-bent on outlawing God and religion.

Our prophetic, evangelistic witness—in our lifestyle and our public voice—is the only hope we have for our children, communities, and nation. The prophetic voice strengthens the influence and impact of our Church in the modern world.

Think of Dorothy Day—a laywoman who had a great love for justice. She founded the Catholic Worker movement, a nonviolent, pacifist association of communities dedicated, to this day, to aiding the poor. Dorothy pursued justice for the outcast and disenfranchised. She had no patience with hypocrisy wherever it reared its ugly head, and she had no need for personal glory. Today this controversial figure is being considered for canonization as a saint of the Church.

The late Fr. Emery Labbe, my one-time spiritual director, made world news back in the 1950s when he integrated a religion class in Erath, Louisiana. He moved the African American children from the back of the church to sit directly behind the Cajun American children. This pastor of Our Lady of Lourdes parish was vilified by the "good" white Catholics in town. One enraged woman slapped him in the face.

Even military personnel overseas heard of the incident. Fr. Labbe forced people in Erath and elsewhere to think about racial discrimination and to recognize it in themselves. Within a year, many of those angry Cajuns were reconciled with their pastor and their Church.

Further evidence of Fr. Labbe's prophetic gift was manifested—less dramatically, to be sure—in his preaching of God's love. Shortly after he first came to Erath as an assistant, Mass attendance increased from a relative few to a full church at three Masses. Recipients of Holy Communion grew in number from fifteen or twenty old ladies to several full Communion rails at all the weekend Masses.

You are not Dorothy Day or Fr. Labbe. You are who God wants you to be. He gives you the gifts you need for the task at hand—family life, work, play, and, of course, sharing your faith. Always remember what St. Paul tells us about God's help:

Since we have gifts that differ according to the grace given to us, let us exercise them; if prophecy, in proportion to the faith; if ministry, in ministering; if one is a teacher, in teaching; if one exhorts, in exhortation; if one contributes, in generosity; if one is over others, in diligence; if one does acts of mercy, with cheerfulness. (Romans 12:6–8)

You are called by God. He does not always call the qualified—but he always qualifies the called. Have faith in him.

HOW TO RECEIVE AND EXERCISE THE MINISTERIAL GIFTS

These ministerial gifts of the Holy Spirit are important. They are given to us for the sake of others. That being said, how do we acquire them?

These steps may be helpful:

1. Thank God and praise him for his goodness in giving you life and the grace of baptism and confirmation. A grateful heart is open to the Lord.

2. Pray over the Scriptures that speak of God's gifts and graces: Isaiah 11:2–3; Romans 12:6–8; and 1 Corinthians 12:4–11.

3. In faith ask the Holy Spirit to help you discern your natural abilities and to reveal to you the gifts you need in order to be able to do what the Lord wants you to do.

4. Ask the Holy Spirit to give you these necessary gifts; be open to them; consciously receive them; thank God for them.

5. Consult someone with spiritual authority and/or gifts—a priest, deacon, nun, or layperson—to discern with you what God is telling you.

6. Prayerfully process that person's input. If you are still unsure, pray some more and even go back to your advisor.

7. Again, thank God.

8. Trust the Holy Spirit to let you understand what needs to be said and done. Don't second-guess the Spirit. Listen to him. If you are on the right track, you will experience both peace and confidence.

9. Use your gifts to do what Jesus did!

10. Always be open to new gifts of the Spirit.

For Reflection

- Do you know someone who exercises the ministerial gifts? Describe how.

- Pick one of the steps listed above to focus on during the next week. Write the outcome in your journal.

- What ministerial gift do you sense the Spirit offering you? Do you have any resistance to this? If so, describe.

CHAPTER TEN

You
and
Global
Salvation

Moral consensus is collapsing, consensus without which juridical and political structures cannot function....

...The very future of the world is at stake.

—Benedict XVI, *Christmas Greetings to the Roman Curia*, 2010

Sometimes even the most dedicated Christian disciple can feel overwhelmed when he or she considers the magnitude of problems besetting humanity. Even the problems of our local community can make us feel helpless and insignificant. Some obvious concerns are crime, domestic violence, and the need to educate our children in order to prepare them for a future in which global competition is the norm.

However, an equally frightening trend is that faithlessness has taken over the government and social structures of our nation—a nation founded on Judeo-Christian faith and principles. There are undisguised efforts to silence believers who want to give public thanks and witness to God. It is as though a minority of unbelievers dictates what believers can and cannot say. They fight, too often successfully, against prayer in

schools and at sports events. They substitute *holiday* for *Christmas* and *spring festival* for *Easter*. The list goes on and on.

Isaiah the prophet gives us food for thought:

> The Lord said:
> Since this people draws near with words only
>   and honors me with their lips alone,
>   though their hearts are far from me,
> And fear of me has become
>   mere precept of human teaching,
> Therefore I will again deal with this people
>   in surprising and wondrous fashion:
> The wisdom of its wise men shall perish,
>   and the prudence of the prudent shall vanish.
> (Isaiah 29:13–14)

We disciples of the Lord Jesus have a wisdom that surpasses that of the modern-day scribes and Pharisees, whose faith and piety are only lip deep. Because of our faith and obedience to God, we can have a positive impact on people in our everyday life—and therefore on the entire world.

In a Dale Carnegie management course, I learned that each person knows at least two hundred people well enough to affect their lives. These people in turn know numerous others well enough to affect their lives. So your influence, like the ripples moving away from a stone dropped in the water, reaches ever outward. Pray that your influence is holy and pleasing to God.

The conversion of the world begins with and continues through the personal witness of committed Christians around the world. When a disciple of Christ lives under the influence of the Holy Spirit, the

whole Church is strengthened. Our common and united mission of evangelization holds forth the light that is Christ. United in the Spirit of God, our global witness gives the peace that is the longing of every heart and soul.

It is amazing how much even one person can accomplish. Remember how Bl. Teresa of Calcutta caught global attention because she said *yes* to God? God inspired her to leave a comfortable teaching position to embrace the most miserable and neglected people on earth—the sick, abandoned people dying in the streets of Calcutta. God honored her willingness to help his poor. He provided her with sisters to help her and many laypeople to support her ministry through prayers and alms. And there is no counting the number of people who heard God through her.

You don't have to be a Bl. Teresa to make a difference. But as did Bl. Teresa, you can embrace each opportunity to witness God's love as you follow Christ and embrace his desire to save the entire world.

TWO EVANGELIZERS

Claudia Sailsman works part-time at St. Edward parish in Pembroke Pines, Florida. She believes that a lot of evangelizing "has to do with listening. People want to be listened to. To live a life in the Spirit is to be a good listener. I listen to their stories and share a bit of mine. I talk about Jesus and our faith community. There are people who leave the Catholic Church and move over to one of those megachurches. I ask them, 'Don't you miss the Eucharist?' I want them to think about that."

Claudia works for the state of Florida in the afternoons. She prays a lot for people, even at work. "We are not supposed to evangelize, but if someone sends us a message, we are allowed to respond. I do a lot of faith-sharing by e-mail."

"John" worked for a survey company that did a lot of business with government agencies. He was a good Catholic man who attended Mass every day he could, read his Bible regularly, and had a good priest for a spiritual director. His coworkers, for the most part, were unchurched or lukewarm Christians. Many of them showed anti-Catholic feelings and ridiculed him for his faith.

A coworker's wife was seriously injured in a car accident. She lived in excruciating pain for two weeks. One morning, as the surveying team gathered for work, a man challenged John: "If there is a God, how could he let this happen?"

All eyes turned to John. He said, "I know how you feel. I often wonder about all the suffering in the world."

He told them how God had given him comfort when his own little baby died. He shared how God had sustained his hope when he was unemployed for many weeks.

"God is good; of this I am convinced," John said. "My only consolation, and in fact this is what gives me hope, is that Jesus Christ, the Son of God, was on this earth. He suffered what we suffer—fatigue, cold and heat, sorrow and pain. He saw his friends and relatives die. And at last, rather than deny his Father—and your Father and mine—he himself died. He died on the cross so that we can be forgiven our sins and gain eternal life."

John told them that all will die someday—and that "if we believe in God's goodness and the salvation won by Jesus Christ, we will enter into eternal life, a life of joy and love and peace."

His coworkers were silent. They never again challenged his faith. Apparently he had demonstrated that his belief in God was something more than a crutch or a fantasy to minimize whatever might ail him. Having suffered their ridicule patiently, John gave witness to the Lord who came to a suffering world.

Both of these Catholics responded to the grace of the Holy Spirit in personal ways. Christ's vision of worldwide salvation is celebrated and given flesh in their witness of God's presence and goodness.

Pope John Paul II once said that any prayer that does not end in action is an incomplete prayer. Your desire to bring people to God springs from a life centered in prayer, a life in which you live for God and want him to receive all the glory. In a word, your credibility as a Catholic evangelist lies in love of God and others and in humility.

You are called to do what Jesus did, to bring into your world the Good News of salvation. In a word, you are called to "do" evangelization.

A BRIEF REVIEW

- You are called to be a Christian disciple totally dedicated to Christ's mission. Live, cherish, love, and serve that truth.
- You are empowered by the Holy Spirit with gifts that form you in the image of God and with gifts that enable you to witness God's love and goodness to others.
- You are richly blessed and nourished by the word of God and the Eucharist and all the sacraments.
- You have the right, duty, and privilege to do what Jesus did—to bring the Good News of salvation to your own world, to share your faith story with others, to comfort the bereaved, to pray for healing in mind, body, spirit, and soul.
- You evangelize where you live and breathe, but you do so with the passion of Christ for the whole world. Witnessing the love of God to even one person helps bring the kingdom closer to fulfillment.
- You are privileged: You share the divine life and power of God. You are strengthened by the shared faith, love, and worship of others in your parish family.

- Now you must do what Jesus told you to do: "Go, therefore, and make disciples of all nations" (Matthew 28:19). Go now! You are Catholic. Be confident! Do what Jesus did!

FOR REFLECTION

- What kind of a listener are you? How does being a good listener relate to evangelization?
- Has someone in your life challenged your faith? What was your response?
- Spend some time in prayer today, thanking God for his call and his love.

Catholic Evangelization in Formation

Evangelization does not end. It is a lifelong encounter with a God who has no beginning and no end. It is for new converts and for tried-and-true Catholics.

Catechesis forms people to live in faith as disciples of Christ. Proper catechesis includes personal awareness and experience of God; reflection on Scripture and its application to one's personal life; presentation and acceptance of the tradition of the Church, including its moral teachings and the Church's legitimate authority; and understanding of the liturgy, especially the Paschal sacrifice and all the sacraments.

The Rite of Christian Initiation of Adults (RCIA), the process for helping people enter into full communion with the Catholic Church, should focus on these teachings. While no one wants to return to rote methods of religious education and formation, there needs to be an organized curriculum that covers revelation and tradition from creation to the present day. The new *Catechism of the Catholic Church* affords us the opportunity to develop such a curriculum.

One essential, of course, is to preserve an atmosphere of open dialogue with catechumens. Any attempt to educate and form people must involve participants in lively and open discussion and shared insights.

What would a catechesis based on the *Catechism* be like? Just follow the four sections of the book.

Section One: What We Believe

"I Believe…"

1. The Two Creeds: Apostles' and Nicene
2. One God: I AM WHO AM; the Trinity—Matthew 28; John 14:25–31
3. The Father, Creator of heaven and earth
4. Jesus Christ, true God and true man
5. Jesus, the Way, the Truth, and the Life—his ministry on earth
6. Christ's passion, death, resurrection, and ascension
7. Pentecost: The work of the Holy Spirit, Lord and Giver of Life; the Isaian gifts (11:2–3) and the ministry gifts (1 Corinthians 12)
8. Life in the Holy Spirit (fruits of the Spirit, Galatians 5:22–23)

Section Two: God With Us in Sacrament

"I am with you always" (Mathew 28:20)

What a sacrament is; the special encounter with God and the Church

1. Baptism: The Fall and the promise, the body of Christ, share in divine life, new creation
2. Confirmation
3. Eucharist: The Real Presence, the Mass
4. Two sacraments of commitment: Holy orders and matrimony
5. The healing sacraments: Reconciliation
6. The healing sacraments: Anointing of the sick
7. Living the sacraments: Extending grace to others

Section Three: Life in Christ

"You shall love the Lord, your God, with all your being, with all your strength, and with all your mind, and your neighbor as yourself" (Luke 10:27)

1. The way of Christ leads to life: The meaning of discipleship
2. The Ten Commandments—first through third
3. The Ten Commandments—fourth through tenth
4. The call to live the Beatitudes: Our desire for happiness, God's plan for happiness
5. Human freedom: Faith and discipline
6. Social justice: The seven principles of Catholic social teaching
7. Forming a moral conscience: Making the right choices
8. Cultivating the virtues

SECTION FOUR: HOW CHRISTIANS PRAY

"For me, prayer is a surge of the heart; it is a simple look turned toward heaven, it is a cry of recognition and love, embracing both trial and joy" (St. Thérèse of Lisieux, as quoted in *CCC*, 2558)

1. Prayer: God's initiative
2. Prayer: Our response—praise, thanksgiving, contrition, petition
3. Scripture: God speaking to us now—psalms, meditations on Old and New Testaments
4. How and when Jesus prayed
5. Liturgical prayer
6. Prayer of repentance and intercessory prayer
7. Overcoming obstacles to prayer

Evangelization Resources

Here are some of the many resources available to you and your parish for help in Catholic evangelization.

CHRISTLIFE, CATHOLIC MINISTRY FOR EVANGELIZATION

Helping others to discover, follow and share Jesus Christ

Established in 1995, ChristLife is an apostolate of the Archdiocese of Baltimore. The personnel have ministered in many dioceses.

12280 Folly Quarter Rd.

Ellicott City, MD 21042

Phone (888) 498-8474

E-mail: info@christlife.org

Website: www.christlife.org

HIS WAY CENTER FOR SPIRITUAL GROWTH

Author of several books, including *Reaching Jesus: Five Steps to a Fuller Life*, Fr. David Knight conducts retreats for priests and parishes.

1310 Dellwood Ave.

Memphis, TN 38127

Phone (901) 358-3956

E-mail: info@hisway.com

Website: www.hisway.com

PARISH CELLS OF EVANGELIZATION
International movement approved by the Vatican.
International Seat:
Parish of St. Eustorgio
Piazza S. Eustorgio. 1
20122 Milan, Italy
Phone: 02.58101583
Fax: 02.89400589
E-mail: parrocchia@santeustorgio.it
Website: www.santeustorgio.it
United States Contact:
St. Edward Catholic Church
9000 Pines Blvd.
Pembroke Pines, FL 33029
Phone: (954) 436-7944
Fax: (954) 436-7506
E-mail: stedward1@earthlink.net
Websites: www.usacells-evangelization.org, www.stedward.net

NEW EVANGELIZATION MINISTRIES
Deacon Ralph Poyo, founder
1106 Jackson Place
Steubenville, OH 43952
Phone: (740) 314-5528
Website: www.newevangelizationministries.org
Website: http://www.newevangelizationministries.org/NEM/
    Home.html

PRESENTATION MINISTRIES

Mark Mussman, Bible Institute ministry leader
Formation of Catholic laity into viable Christian communities
Daily spiritual readings, discipleship retreats, youth programs
Phone: (513) 702-7137
E-mail: markmussman@hotmail.com
Website: www.presentationministries.com

ST. JUDE MEDIA MINISTRY

Fr. John Catoir is an author and preacher. Read his trilogy on joy: *Enjoy the Lord, Enjoy Your Precious Life,* and *God Delights in You.* His website offers daily meditations and a fine bookstore.
P.O. Box 754
Chester, NJ 07930
Website: www.messengerofjoy.com

NOTES

1. See, e.g., *Redemptoris Missio,* 86.
2. United States Conference of Catholic Bishops, *Go and Make Disciples: A National Plan and Strategy for Catholic Evangelization in the United States* (November 18, 1992), 10, citing Paul VI, *On Evangelization in the Modern World,* 18.
3. United States Bishops, *Go and Make Disciples,* 10, citing Paul VI, *On Evangelization in the Modern World,* 22.
4. Peter Turkson, quoted by Greg Watts in "A Mission to Speak Out for Africa," *The Times* of London, November 2, 2007.
5. David Knight, *Reaching Jesus: Five Steps to a Fuller Life* (Cincinnati: St. Anthony Messenger Press, 1997), p. 11.
6. Augustine, Letter 130, 22 (chapter 12).
7. Benedict XVI, *Verbum Domini,* September 30, 2010, quoting the Twelfth Ordinary General Assembly of the Synod of Bishops, Propositio 38, October 2008.
8. *Declaration on Christian Education,* 3.